International Relations as Politics among People

Pioneering a hermeneutic methodology for analyses of global governance, this is the first monograph that makes Hans-Georg Gadamer's and Paul Ricœur's hermeneutic philosophy relevant for global politics research. Drawing on the concept of "horizon" as the element that captures the dynamics of understanding in social interaction in order to analyse processes of international politics, this book shows that what is required is the embeddedness of meanings and ideas in human action and reflection. By advancing theory-building with regard to particular questions of global governance, it reconceptualises international relations as "politics among people". Providing a contextualised constructivist approach that highlights the importance of processes to which people are central, it challenges the use of collective concepts such as "state" and "nation" as units of analysis which continue to dominate international relations but which cloud the details of interaction processes.

The two case studies of UN Convention on the Law of the Sea and Germany in NATO's mission "Operation Allied Force" in Kosovo in 1999 are structured around this contextualised constructivist approach developed in the monograph. The studies reveal how interaction processes can be made accountable, leading to new vantage points of our understanding of governance problems.

This book will be of interest to scholars interested in global governance, the work of Hans-Georg Gadamer, Paul Ricœur and hermeneutic philosophy, the UN, humanitarian interventions, and foreign policy analysts.

Hannes Hansen-Magnusson is Senior Lecturer in International Relations at Cardiff University, UK. His research is located in international relations with particular interests in global governance, focusing on actors and practices at the transnational level and the role of culture in international politics.

Routledge Advances in International Relations and Global Politics

Norm Dilemmas in Humanitarian Intervention
How Bosnia Changed NATO
Yuki Abe

American Hegemony in the 21st Century
A Neo Neo-Gramscian Perspective
Jonathan Pass

The Duty of Care in International Relations
Protecting Citizens Beyond the Border
Nina Graegar and Halvard Leira

The Global Politics of Jazz in the Twentieth Century
Cultural Diplomacy and "American Music"
Yoshiomi Saito

South Africa and the UN Human Rights Council
The Fate of the Liberal Order
Eduard Jordaan

Economic Sanctions in International Law and Practice
Edited by Masahiko Asada

Iran in the International System
Between Great Powers and Great Ideas
Edited by Heinz Gärtner and Mitra Strohmaier

International Relations as Politics among People
Hermeneutic Encounters and Global Governance
Hannes Hansen-Magnusson

For information about the series: www.routledge.com/Routledge-Advances-in-International-Relations-and-Global-Politics/book-series/IRGP

International Relations as Politics among People

Hermeneutic Encounters and Global Governance

Hannes Hansen-Magnusson

LONDON AND NEW YORK

First published 2020
by Routledge
2 Park Square, Milton Park, Abingdon, Oxon OX14 4RN

and by Routledge
605 Third Avenue, New York, NY 10017

First issued in paperback 2021

Routledge is an imprint of the Taylor & Francis Group, an informa business

© 2020 Hannes Hansen-Magnusson

The right of Hannes Hansen-Magnusson to be identified as author of this work has been asserted by him in accordance with sections 77 and 78 of the Copyright, Designs and Patents Act 1988.

All rights reserved. No part of this book may be reprinted or reproduced or utilised in any form or by any electronic, mechanical, or other means, now known or hereafter invented, including photocopying and recording, or in any information storage or retrieval system, without permission in writing from the publishers.

Trademark notice: Product or corporate names may be trademarks or registered trademarks, and are used only for identification and explanation without intent to infringe.

Publisher's Note
The publisher has gone to great lengths to ensure the quality of this reprint but points out that some imperfections in the original copies may be apparent.

British Library Cataloguing-in-Publication Data
A catalogue record for this book is available from the British Library

Library of Congress Cataloging-in-Publication Data
A catalog record for this book has been requested

ISBN 13: 978-1-03-223947-7 (pbk)
ISBN 13: 978-0-367-18651-7 (hbk)

DOI: 10.4324/9780429197413

Typeset in Times New Roman
by Apex CoVantage, LLC

This book is dedicated to Eni, Piet, and Jonna.

Contents

List of figures   ix
List of tables   x
Preface   xi

1 Introducing *Politics among People*   1
   Why politics among people? 1
   Beyond anarchy – meaningful politics in strange places 2
   *Aims of the book: hermeneutic situations and how to find
     them 4*
   The horizon of Politics among People*: knowledge
     and power 7*
   Performances and topoi 12
   Outline of the book 14

2 Hermeneutic approaches to meaning   21
   Making sense 21
   Delineating hermeneutic performances 23
     Competent performances 23
     Performativity 25
   Being 27
     Language and knowledge in hermeneutic approaches 27
     Horizons, memory, and the politics of performance 30
   Meaning and (neuro-)science 32
   Knowledge and the path to knowing 34

3 The topoi of interpretive research   43
   Hermeneutic research 43
   Topoi 46
   Criteria of validity in interpretive research 49
   Proceeding by comparison and sequence 51
   Finding topoi 54

viii Contents

4   The UN Convention on the Law of the Sea   61
      The case: bringing UNCLOS as politics among people
         to IR 61
      Outline of the case study: data and the process of analysis 63
      Comte's positivism 65
         Humanity: making the Law of the Sea 67
         Objectivity: delimiting the continental shelf 70
         Expertocracy: who gets to participate in the endless
            re-making of the Law of the Sea? 73
         Summary 75
      Conclusion 76

5   Humanity and German intervention in Kosovo 1999   83
      The case: intervention and the concern for humanity 83
      Outline of the case study: data and the process of analysis 86
      The topos of "Humanity" 88
      From pacifism to intervention 91
         Founding the Greens 91
         Green foreign policy during the 1990s 93
         The responsibility to intervene 97
      Conclusion 98

6   Horizons of politics   107
      How to deal with politics among people 107
      Hermeneutic encounters 108
      Hermeneutic methodology 109
      The cases 109
      Reflection 111
      Towards new horizons 114

      Index   120

Figures

3.1 From performance to topos 54
4.1 The continental slope and potentially extendable EEZ 72

Tables

2.1	Practice vs. performance	27
3.1	Definition of "topos" and elements of an analysis	46
3.2	Criteria of validity and consistency	50
3.3	Accounting for performance: disclosing meaning	52
4.1	Fusing horizons to (re-)create UNCLOS	67
5.1	The dual character of "Humanity"	89

Preface

Reflecting over the origins of a book that focuses on hermeneutics seems to be a paradoxical undertaking. After all, Hans-Georg Gadamer invokes Aristotle's description of a fleeing army as a metaphor for understanding, which is a process and always in flux. Aristotle asks at what point we can say with certainty that the army is fleeing – once the first line of hoplites starts to move? Probably not, he reckons, because the majority of lines still do not. Yet if we wait until all lines are fleeing, we have probably missed the exact point as well. Gadamer lauds this metaphor but is also critical of it (Gadamer 2004 [1975]: 347; Gadamer 2010 [1960]: 359): on the one hand, the metaphor illustrates the crucial element of understanding: that it is something over which one has no control. On the other hand, he writes, the metaphor does not quite fit because it assumes that the army actually stood fast before it flew. The lesson is that knowledge and understanding do not have a point zero from which one simply takes off and moves forward. And such is the case with the analytical framework and the empirical analyses of this book.

At some point I was interested primarily in questions of collective identity, a supranational public sphere and the European Commission's intriguing aim to foster a "European narrative". It was by chance that I came across Gadamer's collected writings when I browsed the shelves of one of the many bookstores in Freiburg during one of my many visits. Having just attended one of Jan Kruse's excellent methods workshops, reading about the fusion of horizons resonated with my prior experience of Gadamer in one of Barry Sandywell's seminars at the University of York and with what I had learned about collective identities during my short stint as assistant in the *Lieux de Mémoire* project at the University of Luxembourg led by Michel Margue and Sonja Kmec. The result was a much stronger focus of my research on culture and meaning as well as the relation between individuals and their social context. Luckily for me, the intellectually supportive and challenging supervision by Antje Wiener at the University of Hamburg provided for sufficient room to leave EU politics behind and explore new directions by venturing into foreign policy making as well as ocean governance.

But as befits the hermeneutic focus of this book, one is never quite finished with discoveries and understandings. Three anonymous reviewers at Routledge provided substantial and extremely valuable feedback on what was once a dissertation-based script. Their suggestions prompted me to rewrite four of the chapters, foreground some concepts and debates at the expense of others, amend the case studies, and update the literature. The resulting manuscript is an original text. It benefitted from numerous discussions at conferences and with my fine colleagues at Cardiff University as well as the University of Hamburg, especially Sassan Gholiagha, Maren Hofius, Philip Liste and Jan Wilkens. Of course, any mistakes that remain in the text are my responsibility.

As so often, there are many different directions the book could have taken. Some conceptual discussions perhaps warrant further and more in-depth treatment, which will have to be postponed to a later date. But unlike acquiring knowledge and being able to determine at what point a hoplite army is on the move, books have to be completed and submitted to the publisher eventually. They may then become a stepping-stone for further endeavours.

International Relations as Politics among People is probably not the final word on how international politics works and how one can know about it. As I make plain in the first and second chapters, it is not even the first word on the matter, given that many people have prepared the intellectual ground for this work. My hunch is that insights over the role of non-state actors, or rather other-than-state actors, will enrich the academic and public understanding of world affairs. From a normative perspective, this is also a necessary move because current politics in the United States, the United Kingdom, and indeed many other countries in Europe demonstrate that people matter for the ways in which collective entities such as states work. Why one would constrain oneself by researching and hypothesising the doings of unobservables remains a mystery to me. Any research that takes culture and meanings seriously needs to do so by addressing how people make sense of their surroundings and the relations in which they are embedded. If this results in a blurring of boundaries between international relations, law, sociology, and other disciplines, so be it. In the hermeneutic view, a horizon is not the final frontier of some vantage point but rather something that is amendable through fusion or expansion.

Cardiff, Summer 2019

References

Gadamer, H-G. (2004 [1975]). *Truth and Method*. New York, Continuum.
Gadamer, H-G. (2010 [1960]). *Wahrheit und Methode*. Tübingen, Mohr Siebeck.

1 Introducing *Politics among People*

Why politics among people?

Global politics is first and foremost politics among people. People engage in diplomacy and negotiate treaties as well as the broader norms of coexistence on the planet, including decisions about war and peace. They do most of this in an official capacity as representatives of a state or as part of a non-state entity, but also as private individuals. After all, money or fame can buy access to negotiation tables and get the attention of international audiences. The point is that politics is not determined by an assumed characteristic of the entities on whose behalf people interact but rather by people themselves. The practice of global politics is shaped by the ways in which people make sense of the problems that need addressing and by their success in finding common ground with others in the process. This does not necessarily mean meeting halfway and compromising but rather arriving at what those involved consider a shared vantage point. War is a special situation in this regard since it is usually characterised by non-communication, but nevertheless the difficulty of establishing shared vantage points after a conflict only emphasises the centrality and importance of people directly engaging with each other in the shaping of global politics and its governance structures.

Politics among People therefore focuses on cooperation, conflict, and the many different stages between these polar opposites. It proposes a fresh perspective on two of the perennial questions of international relations (IR) – "how does global politics work?" and "how can we know about it?" – by developing an approach based on hermeneutic scholarship. This scholarship comes in a range of flavours, but the common denominator is that human existence, which is also referred to as *Being* or *Being-in-the-world*, is marked by continuously making sense of or interpreting one's surroundings (Ricœur 2004; Gadamer 2004 [1975]; Heidegger 2006 [1927]). However, this is not a unidirectional process, because understanding others, both human and non-human, establishes a relation towards the context of Being and also shapes what it is from the vantage point of the interpreter. In other words, making sense involves making worlds, to paraphrase Nicholas Onuf (1989); knowing who or what someone or something is creates entities and issues that enable one to interact with another or towards a problem.

By drawing on and adding to research that has employed hermeneutic approaches in philosophy and sociology as well as international relations, the book puts knowledge at its centre, arguing that it matters for politics among people in at least three ways. First, knowledge is linked to processes of interpretation, which matter when people engage in diplomacy or other practices. The ways in which they make sense of situations and thereby engage in shaping the course of politics are informed by the culturally developed knowledge they bring to the negotiating table and the knowledge they acquire anew in the course of debates as well as while they are interacting with an issue. Second, and relatedly, the knowledge they create as a result of their encounter may lead to new conceptual understandings of shared problems of human coexistence. Their encounters may be transformative for their own vantage points and those of the entities that they represent.

Third, making sense of these processes from the position of an observer follows the same assumptions about how understanding and knowing works generally, which is known as the "double hermeneutic". By clarifying the basis of understanding, *Politics among People* makes hermeneutic approaches fruitful for research on global politics. To this end, the book develops an integrated research methodology that is demonstrated via two case studies.

Beyond anarchy – meaningful politics in strange places

Once upon a time, global politics was seen as being the outcome of struggles between sovereign states. One variety of this interpretation argues that states do everything in their power to survive by expanding their capacity to initiate or withstand war or by otherwise making sure they are not overtaken by others. Their efforts can include investment in military might or begrudgingly forming alliances. A related, though slightly different, version of this interpretation regards the strengthening of the economy and institutional cooperation as the prime drivers of states' efforts to gain or maintain the upper hand over others. It is said that the prospect of nuclear annihilation ultimately prevented a large-scale confrontation between the world's most powerful states and thereby contained the tension that a competition for resources and gains would necessarily entail.

Doubts were cast over the pervasiveness of these interpretations when central elements that lent them coherence ceased to exist more or less overnight. The period around the years 1989/90 was once dubbed the end of history. However, this did not result in a happy-ever-after. Obviously, global politics continued, but the new constellation of states meant that the way to understand and explain it would now require a new approach. The subsequent decades of international relations scholarship were therefore characterised by a blossoming of a variety of alternative explanations. They explicitly questioned the usefulness of encompassing interpretations of global politics, or grand narratives, instead developing explanations from a range of different vantage points, with different protagonists at their core and with a range of considerations of ethics and lessons to be learned.

The main shift in international relations concerned the two elementary questions to which this book speaks, concerning the workings of global politics and how one can know about it. Whereas in the olden days, scholarship was primarily concerned with so-called unobservables (Puchala 2003), the new pluralism moved towards the more concrete, probing the role of culture in global politics as well as the power of discourses and, relatedly, knowledge (Enloe 1990; George 1994; Lapid and Kratochwil 1996; Diez 1999; Milliken 1999; Grovogui 2001). In this context and over time, alternative accounts were developed: for example, assumptions about anarchy and enmity were contrasted with notions of friendship (Berenskoetter 2007) or trust (Michel 2013), as well as the role of emotions (Fierke 2014). This scholarship starts not so much with assumptions about how states behave but rather bases its discussion on empirical observations that directly contradict previous tales of global politics.

Similarly, the role of standing and honour is being explored (Lebow 2008) in contrast to previous assumptions of security and wealth as the main drivers of state action. Indeed, the centrality of the state as the core category of global politics has long since been placed under scrutiny; Kenneth Waltz's position held that what happened inside the state did not matter for global politics because states would do whatever they had to in order to survive or thrive (Waltz 1979), but increasingly the notion that both inside and outside mattered took hold (Walker 1993). What happens within the state matters not only in terms of who is in charge of the government but also in terms of how society is organised and functions, including family structures and practices of consumption, all influencing the provision of security capacity as well as global economic relations (Enloe 1990). Regarding situations outside the state, it has been pointed out that looking at relations might prove more fruitful (Jackson and Nexon 1999), and the nature of such relations is to a large extent shaped by norms and international law (Kratochwil 1989), as well as the work of international organisations, non-governmental organisations (NGOs), and other advocacy networks (Finnemore and Sikkink 1998; Keck and Sikkink 1998), which together create the discursive space within which global politics might unfold.

Once we accept that global politics does not take place in the perennial confrontation of anarchy but is much more complex, new sites for enquiry become available, raising questions about the workings of global politics. In this regard, the quality of German-Russian relations during the late 1980s and early 1990s was greatly enhanced by what textbooks would come to call "sauna diplomacy" (Clemens 2004: 33).[1] The term suggests that the trajectory of international politics might have been very different had it not been for the close personal ties between German Chancellor Helmut Kohl and Soviet General-Secretary Mikhail Gorbachev and subsequently Russian President Boris Yeltsin. Sauna diplomacy characterises a specific process during which those involved shape the rules of their engagement. Those who are part of the process make sense and, thereby, worlds (Onuf 1989) – a notion which points again to the role of knowledge.

The hunch that international politics is indeed based on common sense-making is further strengthened by discussions of the proverbial special relationship between the United States and the United Kingdom, which apparently thrives through the amicable relations between policy-making élites of these countries

(Louis and Bull 1986), even though this does not necessarily imply comprehensive agreement. As David Watt writes,

> It is debatable to what extent Roosevelt and Churchill ever really liked or even fully understood each other; certainly, neither was always entirely frank with the other. But it is obvious that they established an unusual degree of personal communication and a reasonable degree of mutual trust. At lower levels, military and official, habit of easy intercourse also took root and many permanent friendships were formed.
>
> (Watt 1986: 5)

Similar remarks can be made about subsequent relations between the Truman and Attlee administrations, as well as those led by Eisenhower and Macmillan (Horne 1986; Perkins 1986).

As in the case of German-Russian relations around 1990, we can see that global politics takes place in personal encounters – and sometimes in special settings. Saunas are not the usual location of global politics; most of the time, personal encounters involve people consuming coffee and perhaps cigarettes during breaks in meetings, which enables them to explore options for compromise (Witschel 2003: 77). Even though little is said by IR scholars about the *ifs*, *hows*, and *whats* of this feature of international politics, it seems intuitively clear that conducting state relations in heated and damp settings or around the water cooler is unusual and somehow puzzling to most of IR, because otherwise scholars would not feel compelled to prefix the term "diplomacy" with a defining attribute.

These examples highlight the need to look beyond the formal settings we often find in textbooks and beyond the conventional terminology which obscures who does what, where, and how by referring to international politics as a realm of anarchy and/or by populating it with unobservable concepts such as states. By contrast, as a common denominator of the previous examples, this book argues that global politics is a meaningful process that does not unfold through an inherent force, such as a general strife for relative or absolute gains in a world marked by anarchy. Moreover, it is revealing how the first quotation about the British-American "special relationship" mentioned the terms of trust and friendship, which is a recent conceptual addition to research on global politics (on friendship, compare Berenskoetter 2007; on trust, compare Michel 2013). Together with the anecdotal evidence presented previously, which illustrates that politics is driven by interpersonal interaction, an alternative vocabulary containing terms such as "trust" and "friendship" underscores the need for a perspective change in the discipline that takes account of the close proximity of protagonists and their sense-making practices. *Politics among People* develops such a perspective with a particular focus on the processes of knowledge (re-)creation.

Aims of the book: hermeneutic situations and how to find them

In light of these examples, the book pursues two aims. First, it argues that global politics is made in hermeneutic situations or encounters. A hermeneutic situation is a direct encounter between people who may be in a formal position to represent an abstract entity, be it a state or an international or non-governmental organisation, and who rely on their understanding of a particular situation to seek solutions. Their understanding is based on what hermeneutic scholarship refers to as a "horizon", which denotes the socially acquired experience or vantage points, sometimes subsumed under the label of culture, which are potentially subject to change in the course of a hermeneutic situation. It is to these situations and the shaping of horizons that research should turn in order to understand what is happening.

The horizon that plays out in hermeneutic encounters reminds us that people cannot make politics out of nothing, but what they can draw on limits their scope. In conceptual terms, the horizon "is the range of vision that includes everything that can be seen from a particular vantage point" (Gadamer 2004 [1975]: 301), while so-called "prejudices" or "prejudgements" are the result of what Gadamer terms the *historically effective consciousness*[2] that refers to a particular trajectory of the agent and limits the range of their vision of the horizon – their culture. That said, however, prejudgements do not determine the future trajectory, because they are also subject to change in what Gadamer refers to as a *fusion of horizons* (ibid. 305f.). What matters most in the context of the book is that knowledge in the hermeneutic understanding is process bound.

Because of prejudgements of a horizon, the hermeneutic understanding of knowledge holds that it is not necessarily free of values. Knowledge in this understanding refers particularly to one of several kinds distinguished, for example, by Aristotle. He mentions *episteme*, that is, the scientific "knowing why"; *techne*, that is, "knowing how" as expressed in art and craft; and *phronesis*, which describes action-oriented practical knowledge including a dimension of ethics and prudence (Flyvbjerg 2001: 56–57; Aristotle 2006: 1138b; Brown 2012: 445; Michel 2013). Because it contains not only a functional but also an inherently normative dimension, the examples of politics among people given previously show that it is phronesis which is the central kind of knowledge in this book. In its functional dimension, phronesis relies on acquired, latent background knowledge (Pouliot 2008). However, as it is immediately conducive to world-making (Onuf 1989), it also holds a normative dimension (compare Wiener 2008 for an empirical study). It thus refers to the existing capabilities of people, including their gut instincts, which allow them to meaningfully engage in a particular setting.

Second, the book takes the hermeneutic premise literally and presents ways in which it can be transformed into research. The opening paragraphs of this book thus serve to illustrate that explanation and understanding of global politics may take on different literary forms. While the shift towards (a) pluralist tale(s) of global politics highlights that grand narratives hold little sway and can be replaced with a different set of characters and plot that better fit what is happening, the book consciously develops this technique based on hermeneutic principles.

Thus, the impetus behind the book's focus on hermeneutic encounters as loci of politics and the corresponding methodology is to pave the way for theorising about global politics. *Politics among People* adds to the growing literature on how people matter in politics, which has, for instance, argued that individuals became objects of political and legal analyses (Gholiagha 2015; Dill 2019) or discussed the ethics of leadership roles and the ensuing impact on global order (Gaskarth 2013). In this book, the individual is placed in the cultural context of their current social relations as well as the trajectory of this web.

In this regard, critical constructivists have called for research to pay attention to the manner in which intersubjectively shared resources are put into use in practice – thereby creating and perpetuating meaning (Weldes and Saco 1996: 373; Laffey and Weldes 1997: 199; Wiener 2004: 192). While this research has established that "meaning and context matters", particularly in contradistinction to the positivistic understanding of individual "ideas" (Goldstein and Keohane 1993; critically: Laffey and Weldes 1997; Christiansen, Jørgensen et al. 1999), the question is how meaning can be conceptualised in order to discuss *trajectories* of international politics *over time*. In the following chapters, I advance this point by drawing on the concept of *performance* – a term borrowed from hermeneutic anthropology (Turner 1982; Fabian 1990). This contains two dimensions: first, performance expresses the reliance on a given stock of knowledge during processes of understanding, their horizon, when people *act on meanings*. This is not unlike a recital of a theatre play for which actors rely on a foundational script.

Second, performance expresses the individual trajectory of socially acquired knowledge resources and the fact that, despite being social in origin, knowledge is held individually. To stick with the theatre analogy, this second trait underlines that actors attach their own interpretation to their role and thus *create meanings* during the process of enactment. There is scope for creative agency, given that first, performances are not autonomous repetitions, and second, they are intersubjective. Based on this insight, by highlighting interactive processes of sense-making that may create something new, for instance, redefining German-Russian relations through sauna diplomacy, I will later introduce the term "play of performances".

Hermeneutic encounters do not only take place in the context of performances; they also describe the relation between the researcher and his or her object of study. As a second-order interpretation, the double hermeneutic (Giddens 1984; Guzzini 2000: 156; Jackson 2006b: 267; Hofius et al. 2014) positions the researcher in the process of understanding and explaining global politics. Research reconstructs a play of performances, providing interpretations of interpretations. In accordance with the hermeneutic premise of forever-widening horizons, research results are an account of one's observations, but they are not representative of "a truth" that exists independently of the researcher and is waiting to be discovered.

A strategy to deal with this double hermeneutic situation is to provide a narrative account of one's observation, in which agents and their relations are theoretically reflected upon and which elucidates how certain events in international politics came about (Bevir and Rhodes 2004: 25; Suganami 2008: 329). The expected outcome of such research is a narrative reconstruction which is "constitutively causal" in that it first delineates the inventory through which agents meaningfully created a particular episode of global governance (Ruggie 1998: 85ff; Jackson 2006a: 43; Klotz and Lynch 2007: 14; Lebow 2009: 213) and second provides a meta-theoretical perspective. It thereby accounts for the ways in which a particular phenomenon of international politics takes place and opens that process to debate. Although centring on narrative, the approach here is analytical and thereby different from the recent interest in this concept as a way to describe discursive interventions as "strategic narratives" (Miskimmon, O'Loughlin et al. 2013; Gadinger, Jarzebski et al. 2014).

The narrative account as an analytical device as it is used in this book is not a model of politics, which is the format chosen by positivist approaches. Rather, as Bevir and Rhodes explain,

> The notion of a model evokes a monolithic and unchanging object of study that fits well with positivist attempts to ignore meaning, difference and contingency. [. . . By contrast] narratives reveal the diversity of beliefs and traditions on which institutions rest. They also show the contingent and changing nature of institutions as they are constantly recreated through particular actions.
>
> (Bevir and Rhodes 2004: 25)

Given that efforts aimed at finding nomothetic models which contain causal explanations of "how things really are" have been in vain (Kratochwil 1993: 66), I suggest expanding on the concept of "topos", which Friedrich Kratochwil introduced to IR but which has not received much discussion since (Kratochwil 1989: 219). In the original Greek understanding, topos (or the plural form topoi) denotes common-places containing an arrangement of argumentative positions. In the case studies in the second part of the book, I refer to topoi in a broader sense. Here, a topos is a (meta-)narrative account of a particular incident in international politics which delineates the constitutively causal unfolding of events with an emphasis on the ways in which people create and act on meanings. The topoi I derive from analyses of people's statements and the hermeneutic resources available to them should be regarded as ideal types. They aim "to make people pause and think" (Haas 1980: 405).

Therefore, rather than being a *model* of politics, a narrative approach focusing on topoi addresses the wider question of knowledge production in IR and hence forms a self-reflexive, critical stance within the discipline (Yanow 2009; Kornprobst 2013). While I place the empirical part of the study in the double-hermeneutic strand of IR, the topological approach presented here moves beyond acknowledging the interpretive nature of research. Relating to the critical strand of IR scholarship, topoi provide a narrative account of "what is going on". *Politics among People* thereby seeks to find explanations for "why things are as they are" and thus how they could be different (Onuf 2013 [1998]: Chapter 1). The approach is thus a first step in highlighting potential for change, for example, in terms of institutional design. I will return to this issue in the conclusion.

The horizon of *Politics among People*: knowledge and power

Intellectually, this book is indebted to a range of conceptual discussions and studies that have diversified the study of global politics during the last three decades.

Some of these works will be discussed in more detail in later sections, but even a cursory overview of the state of the art of the art of the state (compare Kratochwil and Ruggie 1986) can outline the substantial intellectual background to which this book relates. This involves in particular questions of power and knowledge that were brought to the fore in approaches that questioned the notion of global politics as an affair of states and the legacy of hermeneutic research in particular that addressed questions of normativity, sought to refine existing theories of international relations, and made considerable empirical inroads.

Feminist and postcolonial scholars of global politics were among the first to rigorously develop alternative approaches to the ones that centre on Westphalian understandings of sovereignty. For instance, Cynthia Enloe highlighted the kinds of questions that were not asked by those interested in global politics and the kinds of processes that were overlooked by disregarding the role of women in state practices and the global economy (Enloe 1990). Her work was among the first to reject positivist approaches on the basis that they asked irrelevant questions. As a result, postpositivist scholarship engaged with practical knowledge and relied on "hermeneutic, historical, narrative, and case study methodological orientations rather than on causal analysis of unproblematically defined empirical patterns" (Tickner 2006: 24). The result was an interpretivist methodology that would be marked by self-reflexivity concerning potential hierarchies of power between the researcher and their subject of study and assumptions about how global politics worked, given that the world is in constant flux (Ackerly, Stern et al. 2006: 7). At the heart of this flux are sense-making practices (Onuf 1989), based on the notion that meaning is social and not something that is just "ideas in people's heads" (Laffey and Weldes 1997; Epstein 2008: 9). Representational practices – that is, words, images, sounds, and artefacts – constitute knowledge claims and are a form of power, because they "attach meaning to subject, simultaneously rendering the concept or idea of the subject communicable" (Shepherd 2017: 22). Akin to the treatment of gendered issues in global politics, Siba Grovogui has highlighted how particular Eurocentric approaches perpetuate orientalist readings (Said 1979) by assuming "the inevitability of the present order on the basis of the supposed civilizational attainments, cultural dispositions, and work ethics of the inhabitant of the different regions of the globe" (Grovogui 2001: 425).

In her concise summary of interpretive approaches to global politics, Cecelia Lynch accordingly emphasises the focus on human experience in the world that this critical scholarship engages with, rather than engaging in a search for cause/effect relations which may be ahistorical and nomothetic and guided by covering laws akin to natural science approaches (Lynch 2014: 1 and 10). She foregrounds that even establishing causal relations always entails interpretation (see also Lebow 2014; Lynch 2014: 14). The correspondence theory of truth, which distinguishes between facts and values/interpretation, cannot be upheld because how something is represented matters for the meaning attached to it and has consequences for action – both in "the real world" and in theories of global politics. Therefore, there is no extra-discursive realm (compare Hansen 2006: 33) but rather the interpretive or hermeneutic circle within which researchers operate: as the reflexive approach taken by feminists and postcolonial scholars has argued for a while, the researcher is part of a socially mediated condition of knowledge production: creating knowledge amounts to narrowing down the choices of how things can be perceived. This means that some meanings become delegitimised, while new ones are created (Lynch 2014: 17–18).

Scholars have engaged with hermeneutics in international relations prior to this book, and indeed with the intention to provide different tales of global politics than those that gained traction in the 1980s. Hermeneutic concepts and approaches have been introduced to the discipline with a view to contributing to normative-theoretical understandings of global politics, as well as empirical analyses. The following paragraphs address these two fields.

Regarding the normative-theoretical contribution, hermeneutic scholarship has addressed various concerns of the role of culture in global politics and how this relates to questions of cultural justice (Shapcott 1994: 57). Richard Shapcott and Mark Neufeld, who were probably the first scholars to argue for an inclusion of hermeneutics in the field of international relations, argue that the approach has a role to play in IR scholarship because it allows for a new perspective on international politics in which actors are no longer perceived as self-contained units resembling eggs in a box or billiard balls. Of course, this is a reference to those strands of international relations which take the state to be a monolithic entity. By contrast, they argue, "knowledge of and actions in the world [. . .] are continual processes of interpretation" (Shapcott 1994: 71), which are based on what Gadamer terms the "horizon" and which do not leave the actor unchanged in the (preliminary) end. Similarly, Neufeld justifies a turn towards hermeneutic approaches by the emphasis laid on open-ended processes:

> The uniqueness of interpretive social science is the insight it provides into the fact that the totality of social existence is an on-going process of self-interpretation and self-definition by human collectivities. Consequently, not only the regulating institutions but the underlying world orders themselves are comprised [sic] of social practices, are themselves constituted by and instantiating intersubjective meanings.
> (Neufeld 1993: 57; Neufeld 1995: 90)

Richard Shapcott has also highlighted how Martin Wight and Hedley Bull have understood international society as a "dialogical experience" around the normative base of coexistence (Shapcott 1994: 61).[3] It is on the basis of understanding global politics as a process that others have followed suit. Fred Dallmayr, for instance, has put forward the argument that intercultural dialogue is not only possible but also necessary for global politics (Dallmayr 2009). For Dallmayr, any interpretive act represents a transformative process because it is based on an active engagement with a source (of text) over time. He rejects the impossibility of transcultural dialogue – which is what Samuel Huntingdon would argue for (1996) – but rather points to Gadamer's comments on the process of European integration and globalisation as examples of ongoing re-negotiations of forms of life (Dallmayr 2009: 32). He continues by linking hermeneutic theory with praxis, drawing on the work of Charles Taylor and John Dewey, whom he praises for demonstrating the public relevance of philosophy, since it is in dialogue that diverse societies contest boundaries of ethics (ibid. 34). The normative-theoretical contribution of the hermeneutic programme thus entails and encourages recognising the limited nature of one's own understanding of justice (Lebow 2003: 358, 2008: 514).

Beyond this normative contribution to theory in general, hermeneutic approaches have also been used to speak to particular theories of global politics and endow them with a critical edge that might have been lacking. Roger Epp follows in the footsteps of Shapcott and Neufeld and has neatly worked out the links between English School approaches and the hermeneutic tradition in Gadamer's terms. He highlights that the attentiveness of the English School to diplomatic practices foregrounds the role of language and interpretation, while also linking it constitutively to institutions (Epp 1998: 50). At the same time, he makes an argument for both English School and Gadamerian hermeneutics concerning the potential for critique: both the English School and Gadamer have been accused of conservatism, he recalls, yet critics would make the mistake of juxtaposing interpretation and critique. The actual point is, Epp argues, that "any act of hermeneutic recollection is potentially critical insofar as it treats the world as shaped rather than found" (ibid. 60–61). Richard Little, in a further assessment of the relation between hermeneutics and the English School, argues that methodological difficulties of how to do research in practice have hardly been addressed in the past (Little 2000: 409). In a similar vein, Piki Ish-Shalom speaks of "hermeneutical mechanisms" (Ish-Shalom 2006) when he uses hermeneutic approaches to trace how democratic peace theory not only informs academic understandings of global politics but also plays out in practice. Because of the double hermeneutic of interpretation, whereby the translation of a text is a practice not just of understanding but also of creating worlds, theoretical concepts maybe become part of reality, which he traces through the Oslo peace accords.

Empirically, hermeneutic scholarship occupies a slightly odd position in light of the prominent rejection of methods, especially by Hans-Georg Gadamer (1957 [1993]) and Paul Ricœur (2004). However, their critique was levied explicitly against the encompassing and exclusive focus on positivist methods in the social sciences that took hold since the 1950s. As Gadamer emphasises that knowledge in general and the understanding of what constitutes progress in knowledge are different in positivist and non-positivist research, he does not speak out against the pursuit of better insights as such.

The fruitfulness of hermeneutic research has been demonstrated in several studies. For example, Felix Ciută emphasises the importance of a contextualised approach to concepts of "security" or region-building (Ciută 2008, 2009), which takes seriously how actors define and enact security, albeit without necessarily taking their definitions as true representations of facts. The task, he explains, is to "explore the 'horizons' within which actors and security analysts alike come to understand what security means as well as what it means to practice security"

(Ciută 2009: 321) Elsewhere, with regard to the European Union's region-making around the Black Sea, Ciută has shed light on the inseparable nature of naming and categorising something, on the one hand, and enacting that which one conceptualises, that is, the "Black Sea Region" (2008). Importantly, concepts and praxis coincide and cannot be treated as distinct – they are part of a double hermeneutic (ibid. 141).

Similarly, Cerwyn Moore has demonstrated the application of a hermeneutic approach to the study of violence in the context of the Russian intervention in Chechnya. He holds that textual sources are the usual starting points for understanding practices because they establish knowledge over and an ethical approach towards a particular subject, which may legitimise conquest and domination. After all, "literary texts are dialogic – they convey forms of knowledge – and are often linked to cultures, particular periods and encounters" (Moore 2006: 181). Elsewhere, Moore draws on Gadamer, Ricœur, and Bakhtin to elaborate on the methodology of an "aesthetic turn" that foregrounds analyses of texts and indeed a broad range of other cultural genres. With a nod to Gadamer, Moore holds that "interpretation and experience of art produce 'play' and it is through 'play' that a living relation emerges which tells us something about meaning and knowledge claims" (2010: 317).

This inclusion of hermeneutic approaches in the methodological toolbox at scholars' disposal remains to be reconciled with the rich analysis of narratives that has been blossoming since the mid-1990s. For instance, Margaret Somers has written about the narrative constitution of identity (1994), arguing that narration lets one understand oneself and others by creating particular relations between time and space: "It is emplotment that gives significance to independent instances, not their chronological or categorical order" (ibid. 616). She continues to argue that "[a] narrative identity approach assumes that social action can only be intelligible if we recognize that people are guided to act by the structural and cultural relationships in which they are embedded and by the stories through which they constitute their identities – and less because of the interests we impute to them" (ibid. 624). Her work is echoed by others, such as Anne Kane, who holds that "[t]hrough emplotment, narratives explain experience, evoke emotions, engage participation, and normatively evaluate courses of action, all crucial functions of interpretation" (2000: 316).

How a narrative works, though, depends centrally on the horizon of those involved. In this regard, Consuelo Cruz highlights that frames of a narrative and associated practices have to resonate with others, meaning that not everything can be represented in whatever way one considers opportune (2000). Similarly, Sanjoy Banerjee emphasises that it is the actors themselves, not the observer, to whom events need to be meaningful (1991). The overriding issue in this regard is the focus on context and the embeddedness of meaning-making through which issues become understandable (Heck and Schlag 2013; Berenskoetter 2014; Tholens 2019).

When I say that hermeneutic approaches need to be reconciled with this literature, I am particularly referring to how the concept of narrative has gained currency in public discourse as well as academia during the last two decades. International relations has come a long way from upholding that narratives are a way to reconstruct events and perhaps distort conventional understandings of global politics (Zalewski 2006), as well as the notion that a distinction between understanding and explaining, between structure and agency, is not tenable (Suganami 1999). More recently, the discipline has developed a more encompassing understanding (Miskimmon, O'Loughlin et al. 2013; Faizullaev and Cornut 2017) which unfortunately has come at the expense of analytical clarity. For instance, questions of how narrative relates to concepts such as discourse and whether they are distinct or part of practices remain unresolved. Research needs to be careful not to create another catch-all category that refers to meaning-creation, knowledge, and power. If we are interested in understanding and explaining how global politics takes place and how we can know about it based on the ways in which people make sense (in general as well as of particular problems), we need to bring in the appropriate tools for conceptual analyses that let researchers reconstruct the meaningful practices of collective spatio-temporal collectiveness (Berenskoetter 2014). *Politics among People* therefore centres on the concept of performance, which brings into focus the hermeneutic situation in the relation between those involved – performer and audience – as well as the horizon on which both action and interpretation rest. It also uses the concept of topos as a way to create its analytical narrative of global politics.

Performances and topoi

Despite the claim by early IR theories that they convey timeless principles, it is clear that they do not represent a reality of facts that can be assessed independently from the vantage point of their own premises (Bernstein, Lebow et al. 2000). How theories "work" depends on what kind of tale the theoriser seeks to emphasise (Cox 1983). There is no room for simplistic cause-effect explanations in global politics because of its complex nature. Accordingly, the relation between those elements that "make" global politics has been recast in recent years, and alternative understandings of causality have been brought forward (Jackson 2006b; Klotz and Lynch 2007; Lebow 2014). However, just because there is no "silver bullet" (Lebow 2009), this does not mean that research cannot proceed and be insightful. The hermeneutic tradition provides a considerable tool-set which lends itself to analyses of hermeneutic situations. It is the aim of this book to explain what these tools look like, show how they work, and demonstrate how they enhance our understanding of global politics.

As explained more fully in the next chapter, the conceptual centre of hermeneutic situations is what shall be termed "performance" (Hansen-Magnusson 2018; Ringmar 2018). It is with regard to performances that we can begin to analyse, explain, and understand what is happening and why. Performance is grounded in embodied meaning that arguably provides a more accurate description of how understanding works, based on research in neurosciences (Johnson 2017). This encompassing approach to language highlights that understanding and meaning are more than spoken or written words. Rather, understanding and meaning are linked to the embodied experience of one's environment. In terms of characterising this research in relation to different approaches, one can say that understanding and meaning are perceived as idiosyncratic-yet-social. This ontological and epistemological standpoint might be misperceived as scientific realist because of its roots in psychology and therefore in the world of experiments and verification. However, it is actually non-positivist because it is still held that there is no independent way to know about the world beyond constructions of meaning (ibid. 188).

Methodologically, the focus on processes requires a social and potentially reflexive account of institutions. Herein "not just formal rules, procedures or norms [are included and considered], but also symbol systems, cognitive scripts, and moral templates that provide the 'frames of meaning' guiding human action" (Hall and Taylor 1996: 947). While IR has acknowledged the role of meaning, often cut short by a general reference to "ideas" (for instance, Goldstein and Keohane 1993), and made references to methodological insights obtained from sociological institutionalism (compare discussion by Finnemore 1996a; Finnemore and Sikkink 1998; Checkel 1999), critical constructivist discussions have highlighted methodological inconsistencies as well as a lack of reflexivity regarding the use of concepts and categories (Hopf 1998; Price and Reus-Smit 1998; Weldes 1998; Fierke 2001; Wiener 2004). Furthering the constructivist discussion (compare Peltonen 2017) by refining the interpretive methodology, then, a perspective of global politics as politics among people provides a more accurate insight into how international relations take place on a day-to-day basis, because it is people who fill the organisational settings with life. Critiquing the use of "unobservables" in IR (compare Puchala 2003: 21f.), this book holds that macro concepts such as "the state" merely exist as a result of micro-level interactions – "collectivities have their life in through [sic] their praxiological instantiations" (Coulter 2001: 36). It is there that people create and act on meanings, shaping the trajectory of politics.

In addition to advancing IR theory, the book also enables a broader public debate on contemporary global governance. Following the reasoning that research needs to make sense of the way people act on and create meanings (that is, based on a double hermeneutic approach), a second line of argument is that the interpretive account formulated in "topoi" allows scholars to decentre institutions (Bevir and Rhodes 2010: 90). This not only entails a rejection of the idea that institutions somehow determine behaviour; the argument also suggests that, via topoi, *Politics among People* provides an account of how those institutions are filled with life. This concept provides a narrative to make sense of other people's sense-making, as it were, by accounting for who makes international politics meaningful and how. The concept of topos illuminates the rules of use of [macro-]categories as they develop over time. A topos thus sheds light on the way for a debate on particular phenomena of contemporary global governance. The topos is therefore an important new concept in the analysis of global politics, which the book seeks to introduce with reference to exploratory cases.

Two case studies will demonstrate the role of performance in hermeneutic situations and how it can be fruitfully analysed for a better understanding of global politics. Regarding the UN Convention on the Law of the Sea, background information retrieved by informal interviews – on file with the author – suggests that if not sauna diplomacy, then at least late-night meetings in the UN canteen or Mediterranean restaurants were conducive to developing a meaningful framework for ocean governance. The information supports statements on record according to which a so-called "Gentlemen's Agreement" and informal working arrangements were conducive to trust-building and the progress of the convention text. I hold that the emergence and workings of the Law of the Sea convention can be explained by the topos of "Comtean Positivism", which is built on central elements of humanity, expertocracy, and objectivity. Since more data is publicly available in this area than there is concerning Russian-German sauna diplomacy, the case is well suited to illustrate how politics among people drives global politics and to analyse the development of the Law of the Sea.

The second case, which discusses German involvement in military operations in the late 1990s, takes the argument further. It sheds light on issues surrounding German military policy – which is puzzling because of a lack of such policies in previous decades, as well as a lack of incentives such as security or wealth, and, last, in particular because of the anti-military past of a large section of the governing parties at the time. Nevertheless, as explained by the topos of "Humanity", policy making took a markedly different turn from previous decades.

Taken together, both cases illustrate how performances in hermeneutic situations shape not only knowledge about the world but also the identity of those involved. Such an identitarian dimension of knowledge matters profoundly for agency – but it is not easily manageable because the way the process unfolds cannot be anticipated. Taken together, both cases exemplify how performance, as the knowledge-based process of sense-making, contributes to the continuous instantiation and alteration of global politics. The approach to international relations as politics among people developed in this book thus holds that if we, as researchers, can reconstruct which knowledge matters and in what ways, we are better able to make sense of the phenomenon in question.

Outline of the book

Chapters 2 and 3 explain the methodology of the book. The next chapter discusses the concept of performance in terms of embodied experience and distinguishes its use from poststructural and practice-turn-based accounts. Performance is linked to the hermeneutic approach, especially the writings of Gadamer and Ricœur, and the insights that meaning is contextually bound and independent knowledge of a situation is impossible to obtain. Chapter 3 uses these discussions to unfold a hermeneutic research methodology. It introduces the concept of topos as a way to account for performances. It also establishes some criteria of validity for interpretive analyses.

Chapter 4 presents the first of two case studies. The chapter outlines the contours of "Comtean Positivism", which it argues is at the centre of how ocean governance got its present form. The chapter sketches the social theory of August Comte in order to then discuss three core elements of Comte's writings: humanity refers to the idea that the oceans are a space for all of humankind to benefit from, objectivity suggests that this space is somehow comprehensible in terms of natural givens, and expertocracy describes the mode in which this comprehension takes place. The argument in this chapter is that we are witnessing a gradual depoliticisation of ocean governance because central institutions lack the potential to challenge knowledge claims, and there is little in terms of accountability for those involved.

Chapter 5 addresses the puzzling German involvement in the 1999 NATO intervention in Kosovo. The central topos of "Humanity", however, accounts for how it was possible that a government of Social Democrats, and especially the Green Party, came to participate in unprecedented foreign policy missions. The chapter shows that global norms require a particular ethics of decision-making and do not perpetuate themselves automatically. The case is a small but important episode in the general understanding of sovereignty in global politics.

Chapter 6 finishes by highlighting the role of hermeneutic encounters for global politics and how these should be studied from an interpretive perspective. After recapitulating the empirical cases and their general lessons, I close with a reflection on the limits of the study and an outlook for further research in other governance fields, discussing different research interests and conceptual dialogue with related theoretical vantage points.

Notes

1 The term is also used in the context of Finnish foreign policy by Ferreira-Pereira (2007: 62).
2 The German term is *wirkungsgeschichtliches Bewusstsein*.
3 Compare Kaczmarska (2018) for a critical discussion of the reification of English School concepts.

References

Ackerly, B. A., M. Stern and J. True (2006). Feminism Meets International Relations: Some Methodological Issues. *Feminist Methodologies for International Relations*. B. A. Ackerly, M. Stern and J. True. Cambridge, Cambridge University Press: 1–16.
Aristotle (2006). *Nikomachische Ethik*. Reinbeck, Rowohlt.
Banerjee, S. (1991). Reproduction of Subjects in Historical Structures: Attribution, Identity, and Emotion in the Early Cold War. *International Studies Quarterly* 31(1): 19–37.
Berenskoetter, F. (2007). Friends, There Are No Friends? An Intimate Reframing of the International. *Millennium: Journal of International Studies* 35(3): 647–676.
Berenskoetter, F. (2014). Parameters of a National Biography. *European Journal of International Relations* 20(1): 262–288.
Bernstein, S., R. N. Lebow, J. Gross Stein and S. Weber (2000). God Gave Physics the Easy Problems: Adapting Social Science to an Unpredictable World. *European Journal of International Relations* 6(1): 43–76.

Bevir, M. and R. A. W. Rhodes (2004). *Interpreting British Governance*. London, Routledge.
Bevir, M. and R. A. W. Rhodes (2010). *The State as Cultural Practice*. Oxford, Oxford University Press.
Brown, C. (2012). The 'Practice Turn', Phronesis and Classical Realism: Towards a Phronetic International Political Theory? *Millennium – Journal of International Relations* **40**(3): 439–456.
Checkel, J. T. (1999). Norms, Institutions, and National Identity in Contemporary Europe. *International Studies Quarterly* **43**(1): 83–114.
Christiansen, T., K. E. Jørgensen and A. Wiener (1999). The Social Construction of Europe. *Journal of European Public Policy* **6**(4): 528–544.
Ciută, F. (2008). Region? Why Region? Security, Hermeneutics, and the Making of the Black Sea Region. *Geopolitics* **13**(1): 120–147.
Ciută, F. (2009). Security and the Problem of a Context: A Hermeneutical Critique of Securitisation Theory. *Review of International Studies* **35**(2): 301–326.
Clemens, W. C. (2004). *Dynamics of International Relations: Conflict and Mutual Gain in an Era of Global Interdependence*. Lanham, Rowman & Littlefield.
Coulter, J. (2001). Human Practices and the Observability of the 'Macro-Social'. *The Practice Turn in Contemporary Theory*. T. R. Schatzki, K. Knorr-Cetina and E. V. Savigny. Abingdon and New York, Routledge: 29–41.
Cox, R. W. (1983). Gramsci, Hegemony and International Relations: An Essay in Method. *Millennium* **12**(2): 162–177.
Cruz, C. (2000). How Nations Remember Their Pasts and Make Their Futures. *World Politics* **52**(3): 275–312.
Dallmayr, F. (2009). Hermeneutics and Inter-Cultural Dialog: Linking Theory and Practice. *Ethics & Global Politics* **2**(1): 23–39.
Diez, T. (1999). Speaking 'Europe': The Politics of Integration Discourse. *Journal of European Public Policy* **6**(3): 598–613.
Dill, J. (2019). Do Attackers Have a Legal Duty of Care? Limits to the 'Individualization of War'. *International Theory* **11**(1): 1–25.
Enloe, C. H. (1990). *Bananas, Beaches & Bases: Making Feminist Sense of International Politics*. Berkeley, University of California Press.
Epp, R. (1998). The English School on the Frontiers of International Society: A Hermeneutic Recollection. *Review of International Studies* **24**(5): 47–64.
Epstein, C. (2008). *The Power of Words in International Relations: Birth of an Anti-Whaling Discourse*. Cambridge, MA, The MIT Press.
Fabian, J. (1990). *Power and Performance: Ethnographic Explorations Through Proverbial Wisdon and Theater in Shaba, Zaire*. Madison, University of Wisconsin Press.
Faizullaev, A. and J. Cornut (2017). Narrative Practice in International Politics and Diplomacy: The Case of the Crimean Crisis. *Journal of International Relations and Development* **20**(3): 578–604.
Ferreira-Pereira, L. C. (2007). *Inside the Fence but Outside the Walls*. Bern, Peter Lang.
Fierke, K. M. (2001). Critical Methodology and Constructivism. *Constructing International Relations: The Next Generation*. K. Fierke and K. E. Jørgensen. Armonk, New York and London, M. E. Sharpe: 115–135.
Fierke, K. M. (2014). Emotion and Intentionality. *International Theory: A Journal of International Politics, Law and Philosophy* **6**(3): 563–567.
Finnemore, M. (1996a). Norms, Culture and World Politics: Insights from Sociology's Institutionalism. *International Organization* **50**(2): 325–347.
Finnemore, M. and K. Sikkink (1998). International Norm Dynamics and Political Change. *International Organization* **52**(4): 887–917.

Flyvbjerg, B. (2001). *Making Social Science Matter: Why Social Inquiry Fails and How It Can Succeed Again*. Cambridge, Cambridge University Press.

Gadamer, H-G. (1957 [1993]). *Was Ist Wahrheit?* Tübingen, Mohr Siebeck: 44–56.

Gadamer, H-G. (2004 [1975]). *Truth and Method*. New York, Continuum.

Gadinger, F., S. Jarzebski and T. Yildiz, Eds. (2014). *Politische Narrative*. Wiesbaden, Springer VS.

Gaskarth, J. (2013). Interpreting Ethical Foreign Policy: Traditions and Dilemmas for Policymakers. *British Journal of Politics and International Relations* **15**(2): 191–209.

George, J. (1994). *Discourses of Global Politics: A Critical (Re)Introduction to International Relations*. Boulder, CO, Lynne Rienner Publishers.

Gholiagha, S. (2015). 'To Prevent Future Kosovos and Future Rwandas': A Critical Constructivist View of the Responsibility to Protect. *The International Journal of Human Rights* **19**(8): 1074–1097.

Giddens, A. (1984). *The Constitution of Society: Outline of a Theory of Structuration*. Cambridge, Polity Press.

Goldstein, J. and A. R. O. Keohane (1993). Ideas and Foreign Policy: An Analytical Framework. *Ideas and Foreign Policy: Beliefs, Institutions, and Political Change*. J. Goldstein and R. O. Keohane. Ithaca, Cornell University Press: 3–30.

Grovogui, S. N. Z. (2001). Come to Africa: A Hermeneutics of Race in International Theory. *Alternatives* **26**(4): 425–448.

Guzzini, S. (2000). A Reconstruction of Constructivism in International Relations. *European Journal of International Relations* **6**(2): 147–182.

Haas, E. B. (1980). Why Collaborate? Issue-Linkage and International Regimes. *World Politics* **32**(3): 357–405.

Hall, P. and R. Taylor (1996). Political Science and the Three New Institutionalisms. *Political Studies* **44**(4): 936–957.

Hansen, L. (2006). *Security as Practice: Discourse Analysis and the Bosnian War*. London, Routledge.

Hansen-Magnusson, H. (2018). Arctic Geopoetics: Russian Politics at the North Pole. *Cooperation and Conflict*. https://doi.org/10.1177/0010836718815526.

Heck, A. and G. Schlag (2013). Securitizing Images: The Female Body and the War in Afghanistan. *European Journal of International Relations* **19**(4): 891–913.

Heidegger, M. (2006 [1927]). *Sein und Zeit*. Tübingen, Max Niemeyer.

Hofius, M., J. Wilkens, H. Hansen-Magnusson and S. Gholiagha (2014). "Den Schleier lichten? Kritische Normenforschung, Freiheit und Gleichberechtigung im Kontext des "Arabischen Frühlings"." *Zeitschrift für Internationale Beziehungen* **21**(2): 85–107.

Hopf, T. (1998). The Promise of Constructivism in International Relations Theory. *International Security* **23**(1): 171–200.

Horne, A. (1986). *The Macmillan Years and Afterwards*. W. R. Louis and H. Bull. Oxford, Clarendon Press: 87–102.

Huntington, S. P. (1996). *The Clash of Civilization and the Remaking of World Order*. New York, Simon & Schuster.

Ish-Shalom, P. (2006). Theory as a Hermeneutical Mechanism: The Democratic-Peace Thesis and the Politics of Democratization. *European Journal of International Relations* **12**(4): 565–598.

Jackson, P. T. (2006a). *Civilizing the Enemy: Germany's Reconstruction and the Invention of the West*. Ann Arbor, MI, University of Michigan Press.

Jackson, P. T. (2006b). Making Sense of Making Sense: Configurational Analysis and the Double Hermeneutic. *Interpretation and Method: Empirical Research Methods and the Interpretive Turn*. D. Yanow and P. Schwartz-Shea. Armonk, NY, M. E. Sharpe: 264–280.

Jackson, P. T. and D. H. Nexon (1999). Relations Before States: Substance, Process and the Study of World Politics. *European Journal of International Relations* **5**(3): 291–332.

Johnson, M. (2017). *Embodied Mind, Meaning and Reason – How Our Bodies Give Rise to Understanding*. Chicago, Chicago University Press.

Kaczmarska, K. (2018). Reification in IR: The Process and Consequences of Reifying the Idea of International Society. *International Studies Review*. https://doi.org/10.1093/isr/viy016.

Kane, A. (2000). Reconstructing Culture in Historical Explanation: Narratives as Cultural Structure and Practice. *History and Theory* **39**(3): 311–300.

Keck, M. F. and K. Sikkink (1998). Transnational Advocacy Networks in the Movement Society. *The Social Movement Society: Contentious Politics for a New Century*. D. S. Meyer and S. Tarrow. Lanham, Boulder, CO, New York and Oxford, Rowman & Littlefield Publishers: 217–238.

Klotz, A. and C. Lynch (2007). *Strategies for Research in Constructivist International Relations*. Armonk and London, M. E. Sharpe.

Kornprobst, M. (2013). When the Discipline Is Not Enough – Scholarship, Communication, and Power. *Paper Prepared for Presentation at the 8th International Interpretive Policy Analysis Conference (IPA) in Vienna (3–5 July 2013)* [on file with the author].

Kratochwil, F. (1989). *Rules, Norms, and Decisions: On the Conditions of Practical and Legal Reasoning in International Relations and Domestic Affairs*. Cambridge, Cambridge University Press.

Kratochwil, F. (1993). The Embarrassment of Changes: Neorealism As the Science of Realpolitik Without Politics. *Review of International Studies* **19**(1): 63–80.

Kratochwil, F. and J. G. Ruggie (1986). International Organization: A State of the Art on an Art of the State. *International Organization* **40**(4): 753–775.

Laffey, M. and J. Weldes (1997). Beyond Belief: Ideas and Symbolic Technologies in International Relations. *European Journal of International Relations* **3**(2): 193–237.

Lapid, Y. and F. Kratochwil (1996). *The Return of Culture and Identity in IR Theory*. Boulder, CO, Lynne Rienner.

Lebow, R. N. (2003). *The Tragic Vision of Politics: Ethics, Interest and Orders*. Cambridge, Cambridge University Press.

Lebow, R. N. (2008). *A Cultural Theory of International Relations*. Cambridge, Cambridge University Press.

Lebow, R. N. (2009). Constitutive Causality: Imagined Spaces and Political Practices. *Millennium – Journal of International Relations* **38**(2): 211–239.

Lebow, R. N. (2014). *Constructing Cause in International Relations*. New York, Cambridge University Press.

Little, R. (2000). The English School's Contribution to the Study of International Relations. *European Journal of International Relations* **6**(3): 395–422.

Louis, W. R. and H. Bull, Eds. (1986). *The 'Special Relationship': Anglo-American Relations Since 1945*. Oxford, Clarendon Press.

Lynch, C. (2014). *Interpreting International Relations*. New York and London, Routledge.

Michel, T. (2013). Time to Get Emotional: Phronetic Reflections on the Concept of Trust in International Relations. *European Journal of International Relations* **19**(4): 869–890.

Milliken, J. (1999). The Study of Discourse in International Relations: A Critique of Research and Methods. *European Journal of International Relations* **5**(2): 225–254.

Miskimmon, A., O'Loughlin, B. and Ruselle, L. (2013). *Strategic Narratives: Communication Power and the New World Order*. New York, Routledge.

Moore, C. (2006). Reading the Hermeneutics of Violence: The Literary Turn and Chechnya. *Global Society* **20**(2): 179–198.

Moore, C. (2010). On Cruelty: Literature, Aesthetics and Global Politics. *Global Society* **24**(3): 311–329.
Neufeld, M. (1993). Interpretation and the 'Science' of International Relations. *Review of International Studies* **19**(1): 39–61.
Neufeld, M. (1995). *The Restructuring of International Relations Theory*. Cambridge, Cambridge University Press.
Onuf, N. (1989). *World of Our Making: Rules and Rule in Social Theory and International Relations*. Columbia, University of South Carolina Press.
Onuf, N. (2013 [1998]). Constructivism: A User's Manual. *Making Sense, Making Worlds: Constructivism in Social Theory and International Relations*. N. Onuf. London, Routledge: 3–21.
Peltonen, H. (2017). A Tale of Two Cognitions: The Evolution of Social Constructivism in International Relations. *Revista Brasileira de Politica Internacional* **60**(1): 1–18.
Perkins, B. (1986). Unequal Partners: The Truman Administration and Great Britain. *The Special Relationship: Anglo-American Relations Since 1945*. W. R. Louis and H. Bull. Oxford, Clarendon Press: 43–64.
Pouliot, V. (2008). The Logic of Practicality: A Theory of Practice of Security Communities. *International Organization* **62**(2): 257–288.
Price, R. and C. Reus-Smit (1998). Dangerous Liaisons? Critical International Theory and Constructivism. *European Journal of International Relations* **4**(3): 259–294.
Puchala, D. (2003). *Theory and History in International Relations*. New York and London, Routledge.
Ricœur, P. (2004). *Memory, History, Forgetting*. Chicago and London, University of Chicago Press.
Ringmar, E. (2018). The Problem with Performativity: Comments on the Contributions. *Journal of International Relations and Development*. Online First. https://doi.org/10.1057/s41268-018-0159-8.
Ruggie, J. G. (1998). *Constructing the World Polity: Essays on International Institutionalization*. London and New York, Routledge.
Said, E. (1979). *Orientalism*. New York, Vintage.
Shapcott, R. (1994). Conversation and Coexistence: Gadamer and the Interpretation of International Society. *Millennium – Journal of International Studies* **23**(1): 57–83.
Shepherd, L. (2017). *Gender, UN Peacebuilding, and the Politics of Space*. Oxford, Oxford University Press.
Somers, M. R. (1994). The Narrative Constitution of Identity: A Relational and Network Approach. *Theory and Society* **23**(5): 605–649.
Suganami, H. (1999). Agents, Structures, Narratives. *European Journal of International Relations* **5**(3): 365–386.
Suganami, H. (2008). Narrative Explanation and International Relations: Back to Basics. *Millennium – Journal of International Relations* **37**(2): 327–356.
Tholens, S. (2019). Winning the Post-War: Norm Localisation and Small Arms Control in Kosovo and Cambodia. *Journal of International Relations and Development* **22**(5): 50–76.
Tickner, J. A. (2006). Feminism Meets International Relations: Some Methodological Issues. *Feminist Methodologies for International Relations*. B. A. Ackerly, M. Stern and J. True. Cambridge, Cambridge University Press: 19–41.
Turner, V. (1982). Dramatic Ritual/Ritual Drama: Performative and Reflexive Anthropology. *A Crack in the Mirror: Reflexive Perspectives in Anthropology*. J. Ruby. Philadelphia, University of Pennsylvania Press: 83–97.

Walker, R. B. J. (1993). *Inside/Outside: International Relations as Political Theory*. Cambridge, Cambridge University Press.
Waltz, K. N. (1979). *Theory of International Politics*. New York, McGraw-Hill.
Watt, D. (1986). Introduction: The Anglo-American Relationship. W. R. Louis and H. Bull. Oxford, Clarendon Press: 1–16.
Weldes, J. (1998). Bureaucratic Politics: A Critical Constructivist Assessment. *Mershon International Studies Review* **42**(2): 216–225.
Weldes, J. and D. Saco (1996). Making State Action Possible: The United States and the Discursive Construction of 'The Cuban Problem', 1960–1994. *Millennium: Journal of International Studies* **25**(2): 361–395.
Wiener, A. (2004). Contested Compliance: Interventions on the Normative Structure of World Politics. *European Journal of International Relations* **10**(2): 189–234.
Wiener, A. (2008). *The Invisible Constitution of Politics: Contested Norms and International Encounters*. Cambridge, Cambridge University Press.
Witschel, G. (2003). Nachtschicht auch ohne ständigen Sitz: Die Vereinten Nationen. *Auswärtiges Amt: Diplomatie als Beruf*. E. Brandt and C. Buck. Opladen, Leske & Budrich: 72–80.
Yanow, D. (2009). What's Political About Political Ethnography? Abducting Our Way Toward Reason and Meaning. *Newsletter of the American Political Science Association* **7**(2): 33–37.
Zalewski, M. (2006). Distracted Reflections on the Production, Narration, and Refusal of Feminist Knowledge in International Relations. *Feminist Methodologies for International Relations*. B. A. Ackerly, M. Stern and J. True. Cambridge, Cambridge University Press: 42–61.

2 Hermeneutic approaches to meaning

Making sense

If hermeneutic encounters are at the heart of politics among people, it is necessary to have adequate concepts to describe "how they work". As I will specify in the course of the chapter, the encounters are enabled through the presence of what hermeneutic scholars refer to as "horizons".

The politics of states is the result of meaning-making by people (Bevir and Rhodes 2010; Onuf 2013 [2002]; Hansen-Magnusson 2018; Medby 2018), often in formal or official state roles, who make, re-make, and disseminate meaning through "performances" in the hermeneutic situations described in the previous chapter. A performance is a communicative situation centred on relational links (Jackson and Nexon 1999), which unfolds its effect based on the interpretation (and imagination) of an audience. Performances make up what Charles Taylor refers to as "social imaginary" (Taylor 2004; Taylor 2004; compare Kratochwil 2018: 42). This is not specifically dependent on a particular unit of analysis, which is to say that it can comprise other states or people (Ringmar 2018), although the default position taken in this book emphasises the latter. As Erik Ringmar explains, "[m]uch of what takes place in world politics is not just happening; rather it is made to happen, and to appear, in a certain fashion – it is *performed*" (Ringmar 2016: 101, emphasis in original; Krahmann 2017; Wood-Donnelly 2019). Considering politics through the lens of performance highlights how people draw on and (re-) create meanings by tapping into specific cultural reservoirs and thereby contribute to what is intersubjectively available. The performance locates the performer and those to which they relate in a particular historical and social context.

As shown in the previous chapter, scholars have not always espoused the notion that meaning and context are central to global politics, nor the centrality of people. The dominant research paradigm of global politics suggests that states, and indeed other "unobservable" entities (Puchala 2003), act on the basis of preferences. In this view, states relate to the world primarily through their instincts, especially fear. This mode of being results in a particular behaviour, which is expressed in terms of a struggle for survival. Critics have pointed out that the origin and precise nature of this fear are not subject to discussion (Weber 2001: Chapter 2) and that the focus on fear comes at the expense of discussing other possible motives for action, such as greed or questions of honour and standing (Lebow 2008). It thus remains unclear exactly which stimulus it is that triggers a response from states and whether there are perhaps a number of different stimuli to which a state might react. In other words, what is regarded as fearsome will be subject to interpretation and the meanings attributed to a situation. As far as the state is concerned, interpretation is provided by people in state roles – be they politicians, analysts in ministries writing reports, or indeed in any other official function (Bevir and Rhodes 2006, 2010). Whether fear trumps other motives will also depend on the context. The performance that is central to hermeneutic situations captures this contextualised sense- and meaning-making.

Research that focuses on interpretation and context draws increasingly on insights from psychology, neuroscience, and memory studies to discuss how the individual and the social context relate to each other. These approaches show how context enables performances without determining them, while the social world becomes reproduced and altered at the same time (Wolf 2011; Lebow 2012; Hopf 2017; Ringmar 2018). The key to understanding performance, in this view, is through the concept of culture. In this approach, culture is regarded as a process rather than an object – a reservoir of meanings that may be stored and transmitted through different media, artefacts or objects, but which requires instantiation in practice to become meaningful (Hansen-Magnusson and Wiener 2010). These instantiations are embodied experiences that have a strongly emotional component (Crawford 2014; Fierke 2014; Mercer 2014; Hedström 2018) and are key to how actors make sense of themselves and others (Somers 1994; Kane 2000; Lebow 2012; Onuf 2013 [2002]), including the space in which they exist (Pain 2009) and the policies that they create (Wood-Donnelly 2019).

The concept of performance captures the focus on the relations between people most adequately. The analogy with theatre is not chosen arbitrarily – after all, it is a relational setting of meaning-making (Butler 1988; Wood-Donnelly 2019). The play is based on script that seeks to convey meaning, but each night's performance will have slight variations depending on the actors' input, while the play itself will be subject to a director's interpretation and their instructions to the cast. Also, the audience itself is not merely a passive recipient of what happens on stage. Rather, it is part of an embodied experience in which the audience members cognitively and emotionally participate. Art confronts people with different sensory experiences and addresses multiple channels of engaging with one's surroundings. Gadamer has extensively written about the role of prejudgements and horizons in engaging with art and about how this engagement can lead to a fusion of horizons – that is, new understanding (Gadamer 2004 [1975]). A performance thus combines elements of what will be discussed in more detail subsequently: relationality; the role of solidified knowledge of a horizon, on the basis of which understanding is possible; and embodied meaning-making both on stage and in the audience. Indeed, Hans-Georg Gadamer, John Dewey, and Mark Johnson all underline that meaning-making is not confined to spoken words, but is a phenomenon of aesthetics more generally (Johnson 1987: 164, 2017: 12).

This chapter continues by clarifying and delineating the concept of performance in the hermeneutic approach in comparison with other uses of the term in international relations. It cautions against the eclectic ways in which what is sometimes referred to as the "practice turn" has come to employ the notion of performance. There is a tendency here to advocate the arrival of something new – which I argue is possible because those who present this as a relatively homogenous enterprise conveniently ignore the interpretive groundwork of scholarship that stretches back to the 1990s. In addition, the chapter also cautions against a simplistic understanding of language and meaning in some poststructural work. On this basis, the chapter continues with an overview into the hermeneutic tradition, especially the hermeneutic approaches to language and knowledge that are considered inseparable. The following section establishes the link between language/meaning research and the neurosciences, while the final part reflects on the role of knowledge from a hermeneutic view more generally, paving the way for Chapter 3.

Delineating hermeneutic performances

With a view to providing clarity, it is important to differentiate the concept of performance as used in this book from other approaches in the literature on global politics. Two broader strands of recent research need to be addressed in this regard, as they also speak of performance. They are the so-called "practice turn" and the use of the concept of performance – also referred to as performativity – in poststructural writings. I will argue that the former is primarily a quasi-hegemonic project that ignores the hermeneutic roots of constructivist research while also reinventing much of the discussion of international relations that took place during the 1990s. Meanwhile, the latter approach to performance is built on an understanding of language that is problematic since it is post-human.

Competent performances

Regarding the first set of writings, one of the key definitions of practice in international relations scholarship has been in terms of "competent performance" (Adler and Pouliot 2011: 6). A common point of reference for those who write about practice and performance in the context of a specific "turn" is Iver Neumann's argument that an engagement with practices should complement an engagement with linguistic forms of meaning-making (Neumann 2002). While Neumann himself does *not* speak of replacing one approach with the other, the practice turn literature seems to have adopted a particular path that disregards the nuances of constructivist research that were brought into IR scholarship before the turn of the millennium.

The result is that the alleged foundations of the practice turn literature are too broad to be useful. Practice approaches are praised as overcoming the narrow focus on identity that some scholars developed in addition to, but not in distinction from, neorealist and neoliberal approaches during the 1990s. This allowed them to occupy the middle ground in particular debates (Adler 1997). Emanuel Adler and Vincent Pouliot proclaim that a focus on practices yields a number of advantages, namely a better and different understanding of theory and international politics; a possible avenue for conversation between paradigms; the bridging of divides between stability and change, agency and structure, and ideas and matter; and, finally, nothing less than an "exciting and innovative research agenda" (Adler and Pouliot 2011: 5). This presentation of the alleged innovation is mirrored in other publications that claim to provide an overview of the state of the art (Bueger and Gadinger 2014; McCourt 2016). Among the alleged virtues of the new approach are: an overcoming of dualisms between subjectivity and objectivity (Pouliot 2007); being able to take into account the importance of everyday routines, habitual practices, and background knowledge (Pouliot 2010; Bueger and Gadinger 2015); and a focus that would not value causal over constitutive analysis (McCourt 2016: 475).

The eclecticism with which some overviews of the role of practice in international relations approach their subject makes it appear that any social science approach can be a practice perspective. Accordingly, a brief listing in Adler and Pouliot's introductory chapter features more than a dozen white, male, and mostly deceased Western philosophers and social scientists who are supposedly responsible for providing the intellectual origin of this literature, with the sole female addition of Judith Butler. This list seeks to subsume the entire spectrum of postpositivist research in international relations (see also the discussion in Bueger and Gadinger 2015: 454). In consequence, it suggests a temporal equiprimordiality of poststructural analyses of textual practices and constructivist research that both flow into the practice turn.

However, it is worth reminding ourselves that the premises on which these scholars' respective work is based are sometimes incompatible, and their only common denominator is a concern with the social world. For instance, Karl Marx's concern with life is based on a teleological conception of human interaction in which the distinction between correct and false consciousness occupies a prominent role, while Ludwig Wittgenstein's focus lies on the use of language as constitutive of meaning.[1] Overall, the absence of hermeneutic scholars such as Gadamer and Ricœur from the practice literature is noticeable, as is the gendered and geographic imbalance of its alleged foundations.

The omission of a detailed discussion of so-called consistent and critical constructivist work (Fierke 2007; Kurowska and Kratochwil 2012) particularly concerns the role of four aspects – intersubjectivity, the inseparability of knowing and doing, questions of power, and the centrality of interpretation – which are at the heart of the hermeneutic project. First, regarding intersubjectivity, Jutta Weldes, in collaboration with Diane Saco, argued long before it became fashionable to engage with practices as a distinct "turn" that "we always understand our environment in a mediated fashion, through a process of interpretation" (Weldes and Saco 1996: 368). To them, understanding and engaging with one's surroundings is a social process; consistent with the hermeneutic premise, in their explanation of US foreign policy towards Cuba, Weldes and Saco write that discourse is "a social practice through which thoughts and beliefs are themselves constituted. [. . .] Subjective understandings are derived, in the first place, from intersubjective practices" (ibid. 371).

The second issue concerns the relation between knowing and doing, which hermeneutic scholarship has dealt with in the concept of *Being*. Because there is no unmediated vantage point from which to observe "competent performances", knowing and doing cannot be neatly separated (compare Friedrichs and Kratochwil 2009) and neither can the differences between linguistic and non-linguistic forms of world-making. In this regard, Weldes and Saco pre-empt Neumann's broader conception of meaning-making (Neumann 2002) when they further specify that discourses comprise "linguistic and non-linguistic practices" (Weldes and Saco 1996: 374), while providing the symbolic resources out of which meaningful worlds are produced. All of these practices are linked to power, as the third aspect that the practice turn insufficiently acknowledges, because knowledge creations pave the way for categorising, placing, and thereby creating someone's identity. Jennifer Milliken has pointed out that discourses are knowledgeable practices, which not only help to understand the world but also include an element of power by delineating who occupies which role in it (Said 1979; Milliken 1999: 229). The foundational work by scholars such as Weldes and Milliken echoes Roxanne Doty's discussion of practices as meaning-making processes (Doty 1997: 376) that are based on the contextualised horizons of those involved. In her critique of Alexander Wendt's approach to the structure-agency debate (Wendt 1987, 1992), Doty argues that encounters "always entail an encounter with history" (Doty 1997: 382), which can be understood to resemble prejudgements.

Performativity

The second set of writings on practice and performance is generally labelled poststructuralist. The key reference in this context is Judith Butler's work (1990). For example, she speaks of performativity rather than performance, to avoid a flavour of essentialism. Her notion of performativity is based on John Austin's theory of speech-acts, according to which utterances have a transformative impact on the world (compare Verschueren 1978). For Butler, performance is a *reflected* and *directed* action with emancipatory intent. It is reflected and directed because it is perceived as a counter move against a previous speech-act, thereby aiming to liberate the subjected from an ascribed positioning. Given that such a directed act presupposes knowledge of standards of appropriateness, her approach to performativity resembles "competent performances" à la Adler and Pouliot and is therefore rightly included in the inventory of the practice turn foundations. However, the emphasis here is not on the performer but on the action itself as worldmaking. As Charlotte Epstein has correctly pointed out, such an approach makes it possible to speak of deeds without doers (Epstein 2013: 510).

The privilege of discourse itself, rather than of the people involved, is a common theme in poststructural approaches. For example, Jacques Derrida (1976) argues that meaning stems from a web of relations of connections and differences to other terms. His emphasis is not so much emancipatory but rather points towards the indeterminacy of language and ultimately to the impossibility of arriving at a shared understanding. Similar statements may be made regarding the work of Michel Foucault and Roland Barthes, who share a general concern with meaning, knowledge, and power relations. In international relations, Roxanne Doty has advanced this understanding of knowing and power in her discussion of the "discursive practices approach", which she distinguishes from "social performance approaches" (Doty 1993). While the latter emphasises the "inextricable link between individuals and their social context(s)", building on and reproducing the order of a particular society (ibid. 301), the former regards language as "relatively autonomous" (ibid. 302). It is with regard to the autonomy of language that Charlotte Epstein has rejected the claims of the "practice turn" by highlighting the encompassing nature of discourse (Epstein 2013: 515), in order to rescue the focus of language as constitutive of the social world.

I am sympathetic to the normativity of the general argument, which highlights the relations of knowledge and power, associated hierarchies, and normalising practices. Particularly when Doty highlights the "interpretive possibilities" of discourse (compare Doty 1993: 302), which is based on the openness of language for multiple meanings, hermeneutic scholars would not disagree. However, the understanding of language that informs the poststructural approach is rather quaint. It insufficiently considers insights from neurosciences on how language might actually work. As specified subsequently, research has convincingly shown the importance of embodied understanding. In their discussion of different approaches to the concept of "state", Mark Bevir and Rod Rhodes have argued that a focus on linguistic formalism tends to reify language as an object rather than treating it as a living process. While Roland Barthes argued that "it is language which speaks not the author" (Barthes 1977: 145, cited in Bevir and Rhodes 2010: 72), Bevir and Rhodes argue that the critique of poststructuralists against the deterministic theories of structuralists misses its point. Rather, it is the poststructuralists who "elide questions of whether we are to understand such instability, contradiction, and transformation [of language and meaning] as necessary qualities of a disembodied quasi-structure or as contingent properties and products of situated agents" (ibid.). As Mark Johnson explains, regarding deconstructivist approaches, "[t]here is no way to specify 'the' meaning of a term by connecting it up with some underlying reality. [. . .] Consequently, most deconstructionists (whether faithful to Derrida's original insights or not) reject any attempt to ground language in experience or bodily processes" (2017: 10). In consequence, the state is nothing but a creation of cultural practices that are enacted by people (Bevir and Rhodes 2010).

In sum, performance is the key category through which to consider hermeneutic situations. In *Politics among People*, performance is hermeneutic to an extent that the "practice turn" has not taken into consideration. It is also based on embodied meaning-making and understanding in a way that eludes poststructuralist approaches which regard language as autonomous rather than embedded in interpretive contexts. Rather than emphasising the notion of competence, which Adler and Pouliot use as their starting definition, the emphasis here is on the

Table 2.1 Practice vs. performance

	Practice/performativity	*Performance*
Entails	Enactment of speech acts in accordance with or against norms	Representation
Focus	Illocutionary act ("directed towards")	Reiteration and dialogical engagement ("exchange with")
Can be characterised as	Functional	Phenomenal

Source: Author

phenomenal, on representation, and on reiteration and dialogical engagement (see Table 2.1). In this light, what does hermeneutic scholarship have to say about meaning and knowing, and what is the role of neurosciences?

Being

The approach to performance elaborated in *Politics among People* builds on hermeneutic scholarship, according to which meaning and interpretation are the essential modes of human existence. It is impossible, in this view, not to attempt to make sense of one's surroundings. The entire hermeneutic project is built on the premise that humans constantly make sense, which has induced philosophers such as Hans-Georg Gadamer or Paul Ricœur to engage more closely with those areas of life which proclaim to have specific expertise in the areas of sense-making and truth, that is, science (Gadamer 2004 [1975]: xxii-xxiii). They and other hermeneutic scholars pre-empted the work of current cognitive neuroscience by about half a century, which argues that humans understand verbally and non-verbally – through emotional cues, for instance (Patzwald, Curley et al. 2018). Even though they approach meaning from different directions, the hermeneutic tradition and approaches to language based on neuroscience all agree that meaning plays a central role in how interaction takes place. It is through meaning that people can relate. This is the case not only with regard to human institutions but also with regard to the relation of humans to their environment in general.

Before we turn to the more scientific approaches to language, the following paragraphs seek to clarify the hermeneutic approach to meaning and the role which horizons of understanding play in social life, including politics.

Language and knowledge in hermeneutic approaches

If we include linguistic and non-linguistic markers, the hermeneutic approach to language is a broad one. It centres on "understanding" rather than on the question of "speaking". Indeed, in cultural studies, this has been the preferred conception for a long time, which is the reason the concept of performance, introduced previously, is fitting for the study of hermeneutic situations. For instance, Clifford

Geertz writes about text-as-performance and performance-as-text as two concepts that can be substituted for each other.[2] In this view, a text, in the understanding of "print on paper", does not express a particular object that transcends time and space (Bruner 1986: 11–12). Johannes Fabian has emphasised this position in his commentary on Geertz and, in particular, Victor Turner. For Fabian, both text and performance are aspects of a process of sense-making and world-making. He states that,

> they may relate to each other as phases (when production is considered) or as layers that can be discerned (when communicative events are analyzed), but they do not relate as tokens or representations to events. A text is not a representation, much less a symbol or an icon, of a communicative event, it *is* that event in its textual realization.
>
> (Fabian 1990: 9)

Similarly, performance marks the other side of the coin. According to Fabian,

> A performance does not "express" something in need of being brought to the surface; nor does it simply reenact a preexisting text. Performance *is* the text in the moment of its actualization. [. . .] That performances can be staged, that they can be good or bad, that some people are better performers than others – all this points to dialectical, processual relationships between texts and performances.
>
> (ibid.)

Given this encompassing form that meaning can take, hermeneutic scholars have argued that all understanding is practical (Dostal 2002: 3), which says more about the many different ways in which practices can be part of understanding than prescribing a specific way in which language matters. In this vein, Gadamer has argued that one should overcome the distinction between speaking and understanding, which had falsely hardened since the Lutheran reformer Philip Melanchthon pushed for rhetoric as a specific educational discipline because knowledge of the skills of writing was supposed to be conducive to a better exegesis of the Bible. Gadamer states that "[t]he new science and rationalism, which unfolded in the 17th and 18th century, loosened the tie between rhetoric and hermeneutic" (Gadamer 1976 [1993]: 287). With the development of rhetoric as a discipline in its own right, it became increasingly removed from of the context of daily praxis. This narrower understanding of how language works thus separates expressive forms of writing and speaking from the receptive form, which includes the handling of non-verbal and emotional cues.

As a consequence, and to overcome this dichotomy, hermeneutic scholarship focuses on knowledge as *phronesis*, one of several Aristotelian types of knowing. Phronesis refers to ethical know-how, implying that it is impossible to understand the world without making judgements. It is thus different from *episteme*, that is, the scientific "knowing why", and *techne*, that is, "knowing how" as expressed in art and craft. Phronesis describes action-oriented practical knowledge including a dimension of ethics and prudence (Flyvbjerg 2001: 56–57; Aristotle 2006: 1138b; Brown 2012: 445; Michel 2013). It contains not only a functional but also an inherently normative dimension. In its functional dimension, phronesis relies on acquired, latent background knowledge. However, as it is immediately conducive to world-making (Onuf 1989), it holds a normative dimension as well (compare Wiener 2008 for an empirical study). Even though phronesis is claimed to be a part of the practice turn (Pouliot 2008), it is not used in the hermeneutic understanding that emphasises the inseparability of understanding, meaning-making, and judging. Phronesis thus refers to existing capabilities of people, including their gut instincts, which allow them to meaningfully engage in a particular setting. The point about this insight is to gain a basis for discussing an ethically grounded social life, which potentially opens the way to discuss policy issues. While policy making is not at the centre of Gadamer's and Ricœur's writings, it is worth reminding ourselves that the path to this discussion is opened by their work.

Given that understanding comes in different guises, how is understanding possible in the first place? Hermeneutic scholars draw on the concept of horizon, which in turn consists of so-termed prejudgements, sometimes referred to as prejudices (*Vor-Urteil*). Prejudgements are the means by which understanding is possible and meaning is attributed.[3] They represent a latent possibility and not an unambiguous finalisation and are subject to change and revision. As such, prejudgements can be taken as both positive and negative, as simultaneously enabling and constraining. Only Enlightenment thought, Gadamer argues, has given the term a negative twist, as it was suggested that understanding an object "in itself", that is, in an immediate manner, would be feasible.[4] However, such an approach does not take into consideration the hermeneutic thrownness of Being (Heidegger 2006 [1927]; Michel 2013; Ricœur 2016 [1981]), that is, the position that we cannot escape a process of understanding and cannot shake off the trajectory through which one obtained one's prejudgements, willingly or not. Gadamer explains (1966: 9),

> Prejudices are not necessarily unjustified and erroneous, so that they inevitably distort the truth. In fact, the historicity of our existence entails that prejudices, in the literal sense of the word, constitute the initial directedness of our whole ability to experience. Prejudices are biases of our openness to the world. They are simply conditions whereby we experience something – whereby what we encounter says something to us.[5]

Prejudgements are the components of a horizon. According to Gadamer, then, a horizon is the

> range of vision that includes everything that can be seen from a particular vantage point. [. . . The concept is used] to characterize the way in which thought is tied to its finite determinacy, and the way one's range of vision is gradually expanded.[6]
>
> (Gadamer 2004 [1975])

Commentators describe the horizon as a metaphor that binds present and past (Tietz 1999: 79) and as a concept of contextualisation (Jung 2001: 114) which opens or closes perspectives (Jung 2001: 125; Simons 2009: 35). As a basis of knowledge, horizons are thus closely tied to one's historical trajectory in the sense that history influences patterns of thought and perception – prejudgements – without one being fully aware of this happening (Simons 2009: 121). Ricœur refers to a horizon as a "dialectic of participation and distanciation" (Ricœur 2016 [1981]: 21). In this regard, Richard Bernstein explains, "Gadamer reminds us that we belong to tradition, history, and language before they belong to us. We cannot escape from the dynamic power of effective-history [Wirkungsgeschichte, HHM], which is always shaping what we are becoming" (Bernstein 1983: 167). As Georgia Warnke further explains regarding one's ability to understand art, "[p]rejudices are not our personal property alone, however, nor are the standards they involve the product of our own decisions" (Warnke 1987: 78) – they are rather intersubjective, that is, acquired during a socially embedded process of learning. For example, how one understands art depends on one's *Bildung* (ibid.). Yet history never *determines* the horizon in the way that path dependence prevails. Horizons may include continuity, but they are subject to change – which Gadamer terms the "fusion of horizon" (*Horizontverschmelzung*).

Horizons, memory, and the politics of performance

The understanding that horizons bind past and present and contextualise one's interactions matters profoundly for policy making. In the hermeneutic approach, because knowledge is understood as phronesis, it is impossible to escape making ethical judgements. Felix Berenskoetter, in his hermeneutic conceptualisation of a national biography, has described the simultaneous relation to past – the horizon of experience – and future – horizons of possibility or the envisioned space of utopia and dystopia – as the place in which politics negotiates and contests a coherent narrative for itself (Berenskoetter 2014: 278). From this approach, it is but a small step into the area of memory studies, where it has been pointed out that orientation in time and space to oneself and others is a highly political project (Said 1979; Anderson 1983).

Neuroscience corroborates the conception of bounded understanding and highlights how experience over time plays a role in making sense of the present while also underscoring the importance of non-linguistic and even pre-symbolic experience, such as prenatal infant-mother relations (Mancia 2006). Memory can take two forms, which are referred to as explicit and implicit (Stickgold, Malia et al. 2000), meaning that some of it can be verbalised, while other aspects might be embodied. Even though implicit memory may be difficult to articulate, nevertheless understanding still takes place, and a horizon in the hermeneutic sense forms. Recent studies in psychology as well as biology have shown that there is both a cognitive dimension to memories as well as a physical, embodied one. The academic field of what is called "epigenetics" highlights that stress, trauma, and general environmental circumstances may have an impact on people who suffered personally *and* on subsequent generations (Franklin and Mansuy 2010; Roth and Champagne 2012). This means that trauma as a part of social memories may become heritable.[7] Therefore, the effective history can manifest itself in embodied form *and* encompasses more than merely a personal experience.

Research on the link between individual, social, and cultural memory has long since worked based on the conceptions that neuroscience and epigenetics demonstrate. Aleida Assmann writes,

> Memories [according to French sociologist Maurice Halbwachs. . .] are built up, developed, and sustained in interaction, i.e. in social exchange with significant others. Following Halbwachs, we may say that our personal memories are generated in a milieu of social proximity, regular interaction, common forms of life, and shared experiences. As these are embodied memories, they are defined by clear temporal limits and extinguished with the death of the person.
>
> (Assmann 2006b: 213)

It is clear, then, that individual memories are perspectival and idiosyncratic and thus cannot be transmitted – but given how epigenetics made inroads into researching embodied transgenerational memory and the general social proximity in which personal memories are created, they are part of a larger nexus of memories (Ricœur 2004: 393; Assmann 2006b: 212, 2006a: 24f.). Social memory research holds that it constitutes a distinct conglomeration of attitudes, values, hopes, and fears that characterise a particular phase in time. For this reason, Assmann states that social memory is quasi-synonymous with a "generation" (Assmann 2006a: 27; Hansen-Magnusson and Wüstenberg 2012; Wüstenberg 2017). In its intersubjective character, memory resembles a hermeneutic understanding (Drulák 2006: 152) that is at the same time individual and social.

While it is debatable whether one needs a further typology that includes cultural memory, if we follow Aleida Assmann's terms, cultural memory includes a fusion of horizon with inanimate objects, such as monuments, but also abstractions, such as the "art of diplomacy", which is a political process because it is selective and discriminatory. Examples of cultural memory are libraries and museums as archetypes of storage-memory (*Speichergedächtnis*), but also monuments and rituals, which she terms functional-memory (*Funktionsgedächtnis*) (Assmann 2006a: 58). Cultural memory involves images, narratives, places, monuments, and ritualised practices, but the important aspect in which memory studies differ from, for instance, research on ideology critique (*Ideologiekritik*) is the insight that these objects possess an enduring impact because their meaning is actively constructed (ibid. 30f.). Anthropological accounts of day-to-day interaction make similar points, such as Clifford Geertz's Balinese cockfights and Iver Neumann's description of routines in the Foreign Ministry (Neumann 2012). Cultural memory is a macro-phenomenon that exists merely by virtue of micro-level interaction (Coulter 2001; Langenbacher 2010). Without the instantiation of the individual, cultural memory would be meaningless, as it is through instantiation that cultural memory comes into being.

At the same time, it is in the broader cultural sphere that people find resources on the basis of which actions are possible (compare Laffey and Weldes 1997: 209–214; Tilly 2008). Of course, this insight has implications for the treatment of human agency. While poststructural approaches bracket agency in favour of the power of discourse and the practice turn tends to emphasise the habitual, the hermeneutic understanding shows that agency is embedded in a broader socio-cultural context. Norms research in international relations has provided a rich empirical bouquet of examples on how agency and the perspectives of the people involved matter (Fierke 2013; Wiener 2014; Frost and Lechner 2016; Lantis and Wunderlich 2018; Shadmy 2018). No matter what resources cultural memory is built from, it is through creativity that people can create meaning anew. As discussed previously, no individual performance will be identical to any other. In other words, performances shape the way in which people make politics by bringing their horizons to bear on a particular situation. Given their reliance on horizons and prejudgements, performances are not neutral but rather political practices of world-making.

Meaning and (neuro-)science

Over the course of the past three decades, parallel to the development of constructivist approaches in international relations, the theses that Gadamer, Ricœur, and others put forward in their works have been corroborated by insights from neuroscience and linguistics. It is perhaps ironic that this gives the method-critical approach of constructivism that I develop in this volume a scientific grounding. Philosophers George Lakoff and Mark Johnson, who studied with Paul Ricœur, have written extensively about how meaning and reason are contextually bound (Lakoff and Johnson 1980). They have been at the forefront of debating ways in which objectivist research that builds on a correspondence theory of truth has various shortcomings.

Lakoff's and Johnson's starting point is the embodied mind (Johnson 2017). They argue that embodied experience gives rise to structures of imagination and meaning (Johnson 1987: xiv). To them, the linguistic meaning of sentences, which is referred to as propositional content, is merely a subcategory of meaning (ibid. 1). Rather, propositional content is "*possible only by virtue of a complex web of nonpropositional schematic structures that emerge from our bodily experience*" (ibid. 5, emphasis in original). In other words, prejudgements and the horizon are formed through bodily experience.

They elaborate how the rationality of an argument and its content depend on metaphorical structures which are learned through embodied interaction with one's surroundings, meaning both the physical and the social environment, which echoes the sentiment in social memory studies described earlier. For instance, it is possible to understand the meaning of the metaphor of "physical force" not because of its propositional content, but because we have

> bodies that are acted upon by "external" and "internal" forces such as gravity, light, heat, wind, bodily processes, and the obtrusion of physical objects.

Such interactions constitute our first encounters with forces, and they reveal patterned recurring relations between ourselves and our environment.

(ibid. 13)

Johnson further describes this experience of force as a learning process. He states, "[w]e [eventually] discover that our force has limits and that there is a horizon to the influence we can exert on our surroundings. But then we find out that our force can be amplified and that the horizon of our forcefulness can be extended through the use of tools" (ibid.). What Johnson refers to in this passage is that force can be experienced in various ways, such as:

- *compulsion* through wind or by other people;
- *blockage*, when obstacles block a path or as counterforce, when forces work directly against each other;
- *diversion*, such as rowing a boat at an angle against the wind;
- *removal* of restraint that can be experienced when a door is opened or an obstacle is removed;
- *enablement*, which refers to the capacity to shape one's surroundings, for instance, in moving furniture about; and
- *attraction*, as between magnets.

(ibid. 45–48)

In any of these forms, "meaningfulness and coherence depends upon certain *very definite, highly structured* image schematic gestalts. Their structure is not elaborate, but it is sufficiently distinct to give comprehensive order to our perceptions, understandings, and actions" (ibid. 48). Elsewhere, Johnson writes that "[b]ody-part projections are meaningful because they enact aspects of our fundamental ways of relating to, and acting within, our environment" (Johnson 2017: 21). The idea is that the experience of regular patterns, such as up/down, front/back, balance, source-path, motion, straights, or curves (ibid.), forms the basis of our ability to comprehend the world around us and interact meaningfully.

While the experience of force is prelinguistic, Johnson writes that the experience of force also finds expression in language. Force schemata find expression in modal verbs that enable the expression of meaning of content other than situations of force in a literal sense. Examples such as "you may now kiss the bride" express the absence of social or institutional barriers that would prevent one from doing something (Johnson 1987: 50). While the example of a wedding is perhaps *the* most commonly used one from John Searle's discussion of speech acts and their illocutionary force, Johnson's argument holds that the understanding of the sentence – its propositional content – is only possible based on the understanding of the force gestalt that is metaphorically elaborated and altered (ibid. 58). It is based on experience, which is "at once irreducibly bodily, biological, and cultural" (Johnson 2017: 50). It follows that the structure of meaning-making thus relates to the basic ways of Being.

As an aside, it should be obvious how this hermeneutic approach to meaning and sense-making differs from other approaches that have been used in the study of international politics. Securitisation approaches emphasise that a receptive audience, which not only accepts the speech act but also the authority of the speaker, is part of the model (Buzan, Wæver et al. 1998: 27). However, this approach comes at the expense of interpretation and the role of context (Balzacq 2005; Stritzel 2014; Côté 2016), as do approaches that foreground discursive or habitualised practices (Doty 1993; Pouliot 2008).

The obvious question to follow from this argument concerns questions of individuality and culture. After all, are not (most) people subject to the same basic experience of gravity, force, paths, and movement because of their bodies? Indeed, the approach has listed dozens, if not more, so-called primary metaphors which can be identified across languages. These include the most regularly occurring patterns of orientation (see Johnson 2017: 21) and give rise to specific metaphorical connotations of schemas, expressed in capital letters in the literature: "We understand objects as rising *up* and falling *down* [. . .] relative to our own bodily orientation and our physical surroundings. [. . .] Through our numerous daily experiences with containers and contained spaces we develop a CONTAINER schema that consists of a boundary that defines an interior and an exterior" (ibid.). Schemas that can be retrieved across cultures include not only CONTAINER, but also SOURCE-PATH-GOAL, VERTICALITY, and COMPELLING FORCE (ibid. 22). These primary schemes form the basis of more elaborate conceptual metaphors for abstract concepts "such as causation, will, justice, mind, knowledge, and love" (ibid. 53). Yet even though basic understanding is based on bodily engagement with the world, it does not take place in private. Engagement with the world is socially and culturally situated (ibid. 91), which means that moral values emerge from "embodied, interpersonal, and cultural experience, without needing to be grounded in some allegedly transcendent source of norms" (ibid. 227).

In this view, culture refers to "stable patterns of [. . .] transgenerational social behaviour" (ibid. 92). It is therefore not sensible to make culture a variable for explaining the behaviour of individuals, as people are embedded within culture, and culture cannot be reduced to an individual: "Since thought is a form of coordinated action, it is spread out in the world, coordinated with both the physical environment and the social, cultural, moral political, and religious environments, institutions, and shared practices" (ibid. 95). As we saw previously, leading scholarship in memory studies has long since operated on this basis (Assmann 2006a) and discussed how culture is brought to life through individual and social interaction, not least through the use of different media (Erll 2009), which includes making cognitive artefacts or socially distributing tasks among a group to off-load cognitive work.[8]

Knowledge and the path to knowing

Following the discussion of how horizons and prejudgements form, we can now turn to questions of knowledge more generally. The argument that knowledge about the world is bounded by the concepts of one's horizon has been at the heart of decades of arguing against a natural science approach to the social world

(Kratochwil 1993; Bernstein, Lebow et al. 2000; Lynch 2014). This argument concerns both how people experience the world around them and the ways in which research works. The arguments hold that independent knowledge is impossible to obtain given that anything that is known and knowable is mediated by prejudgements. As Ned Lebow writes, "behavior cannot be reduced to material causes; it is social all the way down. 'Truth' is not a property of the world, but a product of theoretically informed and evaluated propositions about it" (Lebow 2014: 15).

Stefano Guzzini expresses this sentiment in underscoring the indebtedness of knowledge-based approaches to sociology: "[M]eaningful action (and hence also the knowledge of both agent and observer) is a social or intersubjective phenomenon. It cannot be reduced to cognitive psychology or to choice, based on interests" (Guzzini 2000: 149). In other words, action is not individual and interest based because it is only possible on the basis of meaning-making and understanding. It follows that action is mediated through language in the broad sense that was explained previously. The reliance on a horizon that builds on but ultimately surpasses the individual experience makes action inter-subjective.

At the same time, knowing about this action is not unmediated, either. After all, how would that be possible, given that researchers are not able to step outside their own horizons? Research therefore takes place from the position of a "double hermeneutic" (Guzzini 2000; Jackson 2006; Lynch 2014). Guzzini draws on Max Weber when he writes that "[b]asic to the interpretive or hermeneutical understanding of science is that the very human action which counts as significant in the social world, cannot be apprehended without interpretation, that is, without understanding the meaning that is given to it" (Guzzini 2000: 161).

When considered in this light, one could argue that the hermeneutic situatedness might foreclose the path to an independent judgement and to the creation of new insights. However, despite the double hermeneutic bind, new knowledge is not impossible to obtain. After all, prejudgements form a structural requirement of understanding without determining it. They represent a latent possibility and not an unambiguous finalisation. Prejudgements are subject to change and revision when confronted by more convincing evidence and interpretations – confrontations that irritate and unsettle established points of view – as part of a fusion of horizons. The example of understanding art was already mentioned earlier. This position emphasises that understanding is tentative and reason finite (Jung 2001: 121; Grondin 2002: 44) and thus sets Gadamer's and Ricœur's hermeneutic apart from the philosophy of Descartes and Kant, whose approach to knowledge holds that an objective position is possible (Jung 2001: 119; Bernstein 2002: 275).[9] Prejudgements are subject to potential change over time, which means that different vantage points will inevitably be available. Hermeneutic scholars have argued that this change in knowledge should not be seen as a linear trajectory, which is the case with knowledge in the natural sciences and is typical of *episteme* and *techne*. New understandings do not simply replace previous ones in the sense of progress; rather, they offer new perspectives until they are revised once more (Gadamer 1993 [1959]: 59; Ricœur 2016 [1981]: 13f.).

New knowledge comes in the form of abductive explication rather than inductive or deductive approaches. Induction relies on building conclusions from a range of evidence (the so-called "bottom-up" approach) and relies on the correspondence theory of truth, while deduction tests hypotheses based on ex ante assumptions about a research issue ("top-down") and insufficiently acknowledges researchers' assumptions in the design of the enquiry (Lynch 2014: 21). An abductive approach, in contrast to these two forms, seeks to generate plausible explanations from available data. It requires going beyond one's observation and positing what plausibly accounts for the observation in a manner that relates part and whole coherently. As Patrick Jackson makes plain in contrast to inductive and deductive approaches, "[t]he whole of our observations are taken to be explained, not by some general law of which they are a specific case, and not by some general system that they suggest, but by a whole conception of the world that includes our observations *along with* the posited explanatory factor" (Jackson 2011: 83). Cecelia Lynch explains with regard to this explanatory factor that "abduction allows for multiple forms of evidence, pathways to scientific discovery, and forms of causality. Abduction [. . .] is 'concept-driven rather than theory-driven'. Thus it is concerned with the constitutive nature of 'core concepts,' their domains or fields of meaning, and the distinctions among them" (Lynch 2014: 21, citing Friedrichs and Kratochwil 2009: 716–717). Abduction does not aim to test assumptions and hypotheses but rather to develop understandings and explanations, which may be subject to revision at a later point (Franke and Roos 2017: 622).

In summary, this chapter has established the role of performance in social interaction. It differentiated the concept from other forms of use which are either too broad to be useful or lack a distinct hermeneutic dimension. Performance in the hermeneutic approach considers ways of being-in-the-world which are inseparable from meaning-making – an insight that has been picked up in studies of social memory as well as linguistics based on neuroscience. Performance is about embodied experience put into use. While this clarifies how hermeneutic situations unfold, there are distinct questions to be addressed by research, especially the abductive nature of knowledge creation. The following chapter will show how this approach can be translated into a research framework.

Notes

1 Compare Grimmel and Hellmann (2019) for a discussion of the missing engagement of the "practice turn" with the work of Wittgenstein and pragmatism.
2 Victor Turner explains the origin of the term "performance" and highlights the difference in approaches based on Austin's speech act-theory (Turner 1982: 85–86): "*Performance* is derived from the Middle English *parfournen*, later *parfourmen*, which is itself from the Old French *parfournir* – *par* ('thoroughly') plus *fournir* ('to furnish') – hence *performance* does not necessarily have the structuralist implication of manifesting form but rather the processual sense of 'bringing to completion' or 'accomplishing'. To *perform* is thus to complete a more or less involved process rather than to do a single deed or act. To perform ethnography, then, is to bring the data home to us in their fullness, in the plenitude of their action-meaning". While the Austinian version of performance would emphasise the single perlocutionary act, the focus in

the reflexive understanding is on the process. For IR, this means that culture has to be perceived as a verb rather than a noun (Reeves 2004).
3 Gadamer's use of prejudice emphasises the pre-Enlightenment use of the term which did not carry the negative connotation it holds nowadays (Gadamer 2004 [1975]: 275).
4 Richard Bernstein, with particular reference to Gadamer, has rejected this as an impossibility for both natural sciences as well as phenomenology – both of which claim an immediate access to objects, albeit from two very different directions. Both natural sciences, by way of insisting on positivistic methods, and phenomenology, as a hermeneutic approach influenced by the Romantic movement, claim that insight devoid of contextual boundedness can be possible. Bernstein describes such a desire for closure as resulting from "Cartesian anxiety" (Bernstein 1983).
5 For the German quotation, cf. Gadamer (1993 [1966]: 224).
6 The German text (2010 [1960]: 307) reads, "Horizont ist der Gesichtskreis, der all das umfaßt und umschließt, was von einem Punkt aus sichtbar ist. [. . . Er wird benutzt,] um die Gebundenheit des Denkens an seine endliche Bestimmung und das Schrittgesetz der Erweiterung des Gesichtskreises dadurch zu charakterisieren".

Ludwig Wittgenstein, who holds a similar understanding of language connected to Being to Gadamer, likewise points out that understanding is dependent upon knowledge that was acquired previously (Wittgenstein 2009 [1953]: para 30 and 32).
7 Epigenetics researches mechanisms which change the expression of DNA without altering its underlying sequence. Genes are activated or silenced while the DNA is decoded in ongoing cellular activities. In basic terms, the DNA is permanently decoded differently while its sequence remains unaltered. Therefore, epigenetic change induced by trauma or environmental factors is not a genetic mutation.

On the role of trauma in international politics, see Edkins (2003), Zehfuss (2007), and Resende and Budryte (2014).
8 The example Johnson provides includes the use of a 32-point compass to calculate the high tide in a given place, as well as the overlapping knowledge distribution among Navy navigation personnel (Johnson 2017: 94).
9 Of course, more convincing evidence and interpretations offer improvement within the parameters of one's horizon, not an external benchmark. Rather, conventional prejudgements have to be placed in doubt to trigger a new process of understanding (Tietz 1999: 76).

References

Adler, E. (1997). Seizing the Middle Ground: Constructivism in World Politics. *European Journal of International Relations* **3**(3): 319–363.
Adler, E. and V. Pouliot (2011). International Practices: Introduction and Framework. *International Practices*. E. Adler and V. Pouliot. Cambridge and New York, Cambridge University Press: 1–46.
Anderson, B. (1983). *Imagined Communities*. London and New York, Verso.
Aristotle (2006). *Nikomachische Ethik*. Reinbeck, Rowohlt.
Assmann, A. (2006a). *Der lange Schatten der Vergangenheit: Erinnerungskultur und Geschichtspolitik*. München, C. H. Beck.
Assmann, A. (2006b). Memory, Individual and Collective. *The Oxford Handbook of Contextual Political Analysis*. R. E. Goodin and C. Tilly. Oxford, Oxford University Press: 210–224.
Balzacq, T. (2005). The Three Faces of Securitization: Political Agency, Audience and Context. *European Journal of International Relations* **11**(2): 171–201.
Barthes, R. (1977). *Image, Music, Text*. London, Fontana.
Berenskoetter, F. (2014). Parameters of a National Biography. *European Journal of International Relations* **20**(1): 262–288.

Bernstein, R. J. (1983). *Beyond Objectivism and Relativism: Science, Hermeneutics and Praxis*. Philadelphia, University of Pennsylvania Press.

Bernstein, R. J. (2002). The Constellation of Hermeneutics, Critical Theory and Deconstruction. *The Cambridge Companion to Gadamer*. R. J. Dostal. Cambridge, Cambridge University Press: 267–282.

Bernstein, S., R. N. Lebow, J. G. Stein and S. Weber (2000). God Gave Physics the Easy Problems: Adapting Social Science to an Unpredictable World. *European Journal of International Relations* 6(1): 43–76.

Bevir, M. and R. A. W. Rhodes (2006). *Governance Stories*. London and New York, Routledge.

Bevir, M. and R. A. W. Rhodes (2010). *The State as Cultural Practice*. Oxford, Oxford University Press.

Brown, C. (2012). The 'Practice Turn', Phronesis and Classical Realism: Towards a Phronetic International Political Theory? *Millennium – Journal of International Relations* 40(3): 439–456.

Bruner, E. M. (1986). Experience and Its Expression. *The Anthropology of Experience*. V. Turner and E. M. Bruner. Urbana and Chicago, The University of Illinois Press: 3–32.

Bueger, C. and F. Gadinger (2014). *International Practice Theory: New Perspectives*. Basingstoke, Palgrave Macmillan.

Bueger, C. and F. Gadinger (2015). The Play of International Practice. *International Studies Quarterly* 59(8): 449–460.

Butler, J. (1988). Performative Acts and Gender Constitution: An Essay in Phenomenology and Feminist Theory. *Theatre Journal* 40(4): 519–531.

Butler, J. (1990). *Gender Trouble*. New York and London, Routledge.

Buzan, B., O. Wæver and J. de Wilde (1998). *Security: A New Framework of Analysis*. Boulder, CO, Lynne Rienner Publishers.

Côté, A. (2016). Agents Without Agency: Assessing the Role of the Audience in Securitization Theory. *Security Dialogue* 47(6): 541–558.

Coulter, J. (2001). Human Practices and the Observability of the 'Macro-Social'. *The Practice Turn in Contemporary Theory*. T. R. Schatzki, K. Knorr-Cetina and E. V. Savigny. Abingdon and New York, Routledge: 29–41.

Crawford, N. C. (2014). Institutionalizing Passion in World Politics: Fear and Empathy. *International Theory: A Journal of International Politics, Law and Philosophy* 6(3): 535–557.

Derrida, J. (1976). *Of Grammatology*. Baltimore, Johns Hopkins University Press.

Dostal, R. J., Ed. (2002). *The Cambridge Companion to Gadamer*. Cambridge, Cambridge University Press.

Doty, R. L. (1993). Foreign Policy as Social Construction: A Post-Positivist Analysis of U. S. Counterinsurgency Policy in the Philippines. *International Studies Quarterly* 37(3): 297–320.

Doty, R. L. (1997). Aporia: A Critical Exploration of the Agent-Structure Problematique in International Relations Theory. *European Journal of International Relations* 3(3): 365–392.

Drulák, P. (2006). Reflexivity and Structural Change. *Constructivism and International Relations: Alexander Wendt and His Critics*. S. Guzzini and A. Leander. London and New York, Routledge: 140–159.

Edkins, J. (2003). *Trauma and the Memory of Politics*. Cambridge, Cambridge University Press.

Epstein, C. (2013). Constructivism or the Eternal Return of Universals in International Relations: Why Returning to Language Is Vital to Prolonging the Owl's Flight. *European Journal of International Relations* 19(3): 499–519.

Erll, A. (2009). Remembering Across Time, Space, and Cultures: Premediation, Remediation and the "Indian Mutiny". *Mediation, Remediation, and the Dynamics of Cultural Memory*. A. Erll and A. Rigney. Berlin and New York, Walter de Gruyter: 109–138.
Fabian, J. (1990). *Power and Performance. Ethnographic Explorations Through Proverbial Wisdon and Theater in Shaba, Zaire*. Madison, University of Wisconsin Press.
Fierke, K. M. (2013). *Political Self Sacrifice: Agency, Body and Emotion in International Relations*. Cambridge, Cambridge University Press.
Fierke, K. M. (2007). *Critical Approaches to International Security*. Cambridge, Polity Press.
Fierke, K. M. (2014). Emotion and Intentionality. *International Theory: A Journal of International Politics, Law and Philosophy* 6(3): 563–567.
Flyvbjerg, B. (2001). *Making Social Science Matter: Why Social Inquiry Fails and How It Can Succeed Again*. Cambridge, Cambridge University Press.
Franke, U. and U. Roos (2017). Rekonstruktive Ansätze in den Internationalen Beziehungen und der Weltpolitikforschung: Objektive Hermeneutik und Grounded Theory. *Handbuch Internationale Beziehungen*. C. Masala and F. Sauer. Wiesbaden, Springer VS: 619–640.
Franklin, T. B. and I. M. Mansuy (2010). Epigenetic Inheritance in Mammals: Evidence for the Impact of Adverse Environmental Effects. *Neurobiology of Disease* 39(1): 61–65.
Friedrichs, J. and F. Kratochwil (2009). On Acting and Knowing: How Pragmatism Can Advance International Relations Research and Methodology. *International Organization* 63(4): 701–731.
Frost, M. and S. Lechner (2016). Understanding International Practices from the Internal Point of View. *Journal of International Political Theory* 12(3): 299–319.
Gadamer, H-G. (1966). The Universality of the Hermeneutical Problem. *Philosophical Hermeneutics*. D. E. Linge. Berkeley, University of California Press (1977): 3–17.
Gadamer, H-G. (1976 [1993]). Rhetorik und Hermeneutik. *Wahrheit und Methode*. Tübingen, Mohr Siebeck: 276–291.
Gadamer, H-G. (1993 [1959]). *Vom Zirkel des Verstehens*. Tübingen, Mohr Siebeck: 57–66.
Gadamer, H-G. (1993 [1966]). Die Universalität des hermeneutischen Problems. *Wahrheit und Methode*. Tübingen, Mohr Siebeck: 219–231.
Gadamer, H-G. (2004 [1975]). *Truth and Method*. New York, Continuum.
Gadamer, H-G. (2010 [1960]). *Wahrheit und Methode*. Tübingen, Mohr Siebeck.
Grimmel, A. and G. Hellmann (2019). Theory Must Not Go on Holiday: Wittgenstein, the Pragmatists, and the Idea of Social Science. *International Political Sociology* 13(2): 198–214.
Grondin, J. (2002). Gadamer's Basic Understanding of Understanding. *The Cambridge Companion to Gadamer*. R. J. Dostal. Cambridge, Cambridge University Press: 36–51.
Guzzini, S. (2000). A Reconstruction of Constructivism in International Relations. *European Journal of International Relations* 6(2): 147–182.
Hansen-Magnusson, H. (2018). Arctic Geopoetics: Russian Politics at the North Pole. *Cooperation and Conflict*. https://doi.org/10.1177/0010836718815526.
Hansen-Magnusson, H. and A. Wiener (2010). Studying Contemporary Constitutionalism: Memory, Myth and Horizon. *Journal of Common Market Studies* 48(1): 21–44.
Hansen-Magnusson, H. and J. Wüstenberg (2012). 'Commemorating Europe?' Forging European Rituals of Remembrance Through Anniversaries. *Politique européenne* 37(2): 44–70.
Hedström, J. (2018). Confusion, Seduction, Failure: Emotions as Reflexive Knowledge in Conflict Settings. *International Studies Review*. https://doi.org/10.1093/isr/viy1063.
Heidegger, M. (2006 [1927]). *Sein und Zeit*. Tübingen, Max Niemeyer.

Hopf, T. (2017). Change in International Practices. *European Journal of International Relations* **24**(3): 687–711.

Jackson, P. T. (2006). Making Sense of Making Sense: Configurational Analysis and the Double Hermeneutic. *Interpretation and Method: Empirical Research Methods and the Interpretive Turn*. D. Yanow and P. Schwartz-Shea. Armonk, NY, M. E. Sharpe: 264–280.

Jackson, P. T. (2011). *The Conduct of Inquiry in International Relations: Philosophy of Science and Its Implications for the Study of World Politics*. London and New York, Routledge.

Jackson, P. T. and D. H. Nexon (1999). Relations Before States: Substance, Process and the Study of World Politics. *European Journal of International Relations* **5**(3): 291–332.

Johnson, M. (1987). *The Body in the Mind: The Bodily Basis of Meaning, Imagination, and Reason*. Chicago, The University of Chicago Press.

Johnson, M. (2017). *Embodied Mind, Meaning and Reason – How Our Bodies Give Rise to Understanding*. Chicago, The University of Chicago Press.

Jung, M. (2001). *Hermeneutik zur Einführung*. Hamburg, Junius.

Kane, A. (2000). Reconstructing Culture in Historical Explanation: Narratives as Cultural Structure and Practice. *History and Theory* **39**(3): 311–300.

Krahmann, E. (2017). Legitimizing Private Actors in Global Governance: From Performance to Performativity. *Politics & Governance* **5**(1): 54–62.

Kratochwil, F. (1993). The Embarrassment of Changes: Neorealism as the Science of Realpolitik Without Politics. *Review of International Studies* **19**(1): 63–80.

Kratochwil, F. (2018). *Praxis: On Acting and Knowing*. Cambridge, Cambridge University Press.

Kurowska, X. and F. Kratochwil (2012). The Social Constructivist Sensibility and CSDP Research. *Explaining the EU's Common Security and Defence Policy*. X. Kurowska and F. Breuer. London, Palgrave Macmillan: 86–110.

Laffey, M. and J. Weldes (1997). Beyond Belief: Ideas and Symbolic Technologies in International Relations. *European Journal of International Relations* **3**(2): 193–237.

Lakoff, G. and M. Johnson (1980). *Metaphors We Live By*. Chicago and London, University of Chicago Press.

Langenbacher, E. (2010). Collective Memory as a Factor in Political Culture and International Relations. *Power and the Past: Collective Memory and International Relations*. E. Langenbacher and Y. Shain. Washington, DC, Georgetown University Press: 13–50.

Lantis, J. S. and C. Wunderlich (2018). Resiliency Dynamics of Norm Clusters: Norm Contestation and International Cooperation. *Review of International Studies* **44**(3): 570–593.

Lebow, R. N. (2008). *A Cultural Theory of International Relations*. Cambridge, Cambridge University Press.

Lebow, R. N. (2012). *The Politics and Ethics of Identity: In Search of Ourselves*. New York, Cambridge University Press.

Lebow, R. N. (2014). *Constructing Cause in International Relations*. New York, Cambridge University Press.

Lynch, C. (2014). *Interpreting International Relations*. New York and London, Routledge.

Mancia, M. (2006). Implicit Memory and Early Unrepressed Unconscious: Their Role in the Therapeutic Process (How the Neurosciences Can Contribute to Psychoanalysis). *The International Journal of Psychoanalysis* **81**(1): 83–103.

McCourt, D. (2016). Practice Theory and Relationalism as the New Constructivism. *International Studies Quarterly* **60**(3): 475–485.

Medby, I. A. (2018). Articulating State Identity: 'Peopling' the Arctic State. *Political Geography* **62**(1): 116–125.

Mercer, J. (2014). Feeling Like a State: Social Emotion and Identity. *International Theory: A Journal of International Politics, Law and Philosophy* **6**(3): 515–535.

Michel, T. (2013). Time to Get Emotional: Phronetic Reflections on the Concept of Trust in International Relations. *European Journal of International Relations* **19**(4): 869–890.

Milliken, J. (1999). The Study of Discourse in International Relations: A Critique of Research and Methods. *European Journal of International Relations* **5**(2): 225–254.

Neumann, I. B. (2002). Returning Practice to the Linguistic Turn: The Case of Diplomacy. *Millennium – Journal of International Studies* **31**(3): 627–651.

Neumann, I. B. (2012). *At Home with the Diplomats: Inside a European Foreign Ministry*. New York, Cornell University Press.

Onuf, N. (1989). *World of Our Making: Rules and Rule in Social Theory and International Relations*. Columbia, University of South Carolina Press.

Onuf, N. (2013 [2002]). Worlds of Our Own Making: The Strange Career of Constructivism. *Making Sense, Making Worlds: Constructivism in Social Theory and International Relations*. N. Onuf. London, Routledge.

Pain, R. (2009). Globalized Fear? Towards an Emotional Geopolitics. *Progress in Human Geography* **33**(4): 466–486.

Patzwald, C., C. A. Curley, P. Hauf and B. Elsner (2018). Differential Effects of Others' Emotional Cues on 18-Month-Olds' Preferential Reproduction of Observed Actions. *Infant Behavior and Development* **51**: 60–70.

Pouliot, V. (2007). 'Sobjectivism': Toward a Constructivist Methodology. *International Studies Quarterly* **51**(2): 359–384.

Pouliot, V. (2008). The Logic of Practicality: A Theory of Practice of Security Communities. *International Organization* **62**(2): 257–288.

Pouliot, V. (2010). *International Security in Practice: The Politics of NATO-Russia Diplomacy*. Cambridge, Cambridge University Press.

Puchala, D. (2003). *Theory and History in International Relations*. New York and London, Routledge.

Reeves, J. (2004). *Culture and International Relations: Narratives, Natives and Tourists*. London and New York, Routledge.

Resende, E. and D. Budryte, Eds. (2014). *Memory and Trauma in International Relations – Theories, Cases and Debates*. London, Routledge.

Ricœur, P. (2004). *Memory, History, Forgetting*. Chicago and London, University of Chicago Press.

Ricœur, P. (2016 [1981]). *Hermeneutics and the Human Sciences*. Cambridge, Cambridge University Press.

Ringmar, E. (2016). How the World Stage Makes Its Subjects: An Embodied Critique of Constructivist IR Theory. *Journal of International Relations and Development* **19**(1): 101–125.

Ringmar, E. (2018). The Problem with Performativity: Comments on the Contributions. *Journal of International Relations and Development*. Online First. https://doi.org/10.1057/s41268-018-0159-8.

Roth, T. L. and F. A. Champagne (2012). Epigenetic Pathways and the Consequences of Adversity and Trauma. *Trauma, Psychopathology and Violence. Causes, Consequences, or Correlates?* C. S. Widom. Oxford, Oxford University Press: 23–48.

Said, E. (1979). *Orientalism*. New York, Vintage.

Shadmy, T. (2018). Superheroes' Regulation: Human Rights Responsibilities as a Source of Transnational Agency. *North Carolina Journal of International Law and Commercial Regulation* **43**(1).

Simons, O. (2009). *Literaturtheorien*. Hamburg, Junius.
Somers, M. R. (1994). The Narrative Constitution of Identity: A Relational and Network Approach. *Theory and Society* **23**(5): 605–649.
Stickgold, R., A. Malia, D. Maguire, D. Roddenberry and M. O'Connor (2000). Replaying the Game: Hypnagogic Images in Normals and Amnesics. *Science* **290**(5490): 350–353.
Stritzel, H. (2014). *Security in Translation – Securitization Theory and the Localization of Threat*. Houndmills and New York, Palgrave Macmillan.
Taylor, C. (2004). *Modern Social Imaginaries*. London and Durham, Duke University Press.
Tietz, U. (1999). *Hans-Georg Gadamer zur Einführung*. Hamburg, Junius.
Tilly, C. (2008). *Contentious Performances*. Cambridge, Cambridge University Press.
Turner, V. (1982). Dramatic Ritual/Ritual Drama: Performative and Reflexive Anthropology. *A Crack in the Mirror: Reflexive Perspectives in Anthropology*. J. Ruby. Philadelphia, University of Pennsylvania Press: 83–97.
Verschueren, J. (1978). Some Basic Notions in Speech Act Theory. *Acta Linguistica Academiae Scientiarum Hungaricae* **28**(1/2): 69–90.
Warnke, G. (1987). *Gadamer: Hermeneutics, Tradition and Reason*. Stanford, Stanford University Press.
Weber, C. (2001). *International Relations Theory: A Critical Introduction*. London, Routledge.
Weldes, J. and D. Saco (1996). Making State Action Possible: The United States and the Discursive Construction of 'The Cuban Problem', 1960–1994. *Millennium: Journal of International Studies* **25**(2): 361–395.
Wendt, A. (1987). The Agent-Structure Problem in International Relations Theory. *International Organization* **41**(3): 335–370.
Wendt, A. (1992). Anarchy Is What States Make of It: The Social Construction of Power Politics. *International Organization* **46**(2): 391–426.
Wiener, A. (2008). *The Invisible Constitution of Politics: Contested Norms and International Encounters*. Cambridge, Cambridge University Press.
Wiener, A. (2014). *A Theory of Contestation*. Heidelberg and Berlin, Springer.
Wittgenstein, L. (2009 [1953]). *Philosophische Untersuchungen/Philosophical Investigations*. Oxford, B. Blackwell.
Wolf, R. (2011). Respect and Disrespect in International Politics: The Significance of Status Recognition. *International Theory* **3**(1): 105–142.
Wood-Donnelly, C. (2019). *Performing Arctic Sovereignty: Policy and Visual Narratives*. London and New York, Routledge.
Wüstenberg, J. (2017). *Civil Society and Memory in Postwar Germany*. Cambridge, Cambridge University Press.
Zehfuss, M. (2007). *Wounds of Memory: The Politics of War in Germany*. Cambridge, Cambridge University Press.

3 The topoi of interpretive research

Hermeneutic research

The interpretive methodology that I unfold in this chapter stands in contrast to the scientism on which research relies when using unobservables. This was discussed in Chapter 1. Although scientism entered IR in the 1950s and 1960s (Wæver 1996), it continues to matter to the present day, particularly following Kenneth Waltz's publication of his *Theory of International Politics* (Waltz 1979). Scientism derives its basic premise and argumentative thrust from the Enlightenment tradition, in particular from philosophers such as René Descartes and Wilhelm Leibniz.[1] Following Descartes's argument that the mind, that is, the observer, and the objects in the world are separate entities, scientism holds that entities can be observed without any distortion of what would be the observer's horizon and prejudgements in hermeneutic terms. Research is presented in terms of dependent and independent variables, between which a causal relation might or might not exist. This means that the presence of a particular set of causal factors will invariably lead to a specific outcome.

On this basis, it is possible to hypothesise about the relations between objects in the world and test theories that are formulated around a set of general principles which refer to these relations (King, Keohane et al. 1994). The aim of such an "objectivist" approach is to discover "some permanent, ahistorical matrix or framework to which we can ultimately appeal in determining the nature of rationality, truth, reality, goodness, or rightness" (Bernstein 1983: 8). Due to its search for immutable laws, the approach is termed "nomothetic" (Hollis and Smith 1990; Kratochwil 1993; Ruggie 1995; Haas and Haas 2002).

However, as Friedrich Kratochwil remarks, "[a]lthough most political scientists still pay lip service to the nomothetic/deductive explanation and themes, no general social laws have been discovered" (Kratochwil 1993: 66). Sometimes the prefixes "non" or "anti" are used to delineate an alternative position to positivism (Furlong and Marsh 2010: 199) because, in this view, the world may not be dissectible into variables after all. Rather, as my discussion of performance in the previous chapter made plain, we deal with what Harold Garfinkel termed the "ongoing accomplishment" of everyday life (Garfinkel 1967). This presents a difficult situation for the social researcher, who has to distinguish the normal from the extraordinary and make either somehow accountable. There is no way of knowing unless we engage with performances – that is, we observe what happens and we take note of how people create and act on meanings.[2] Therefore, research needs to "study the processes through which identities and policies are constitutively or performatively linked while simultaneously insisting that applications of this framework need to be historically or contextually grounded" (Hansen 2006: 10–11).

In contrast to the scientism prevailing in IR, the common denominator of interpretive approaches holds that world-making cannot be dissected into variables, and it is not intelligible outside processes of sense-making (Kratochwil 2018). The aim is not a discovery of a universal truth, as is typical of approaches modelled on the natural sciences but rather an in-depth explanation of processes. This explanation can be referred to as problem-based theory-building. Building theory from observing the "ongoing accomplishment" of social life, research changes its perspective from "what" towards "how" (in IR, see Doty 1993; Weldes and Saco 1996; Wendt 1998; for a broader discussion, see Kruse, Biesel et al. 2011: Chapter 3).

The methodological debate among IR scholars interested in the construction of international politics has conventionally emphasised its difference to the positivist strand of the discipline along the lines sketched in the beginning of the chapter. In contrast to the linear causal accounts of scientism that pose "why?" questions, the critique has sought to emphasise that interpretive, post-positivist approaches engage with the *constitutive* nature of politics and raise "how possible?" questions (Doty 1993; Weldes and Saco 1996). This distinction follows Alexander Wendt's discussion that casts serious doubts on the differentiation between explaining and understanding,[3] and maintains that the difference between the two types of questions emanates from one's research objective, that is, whether one is interested in change as the effect of some cause, or in showing "how the properties of a system are constituted" (Wendt 1998: 105). The context-sensitive analyses of consistent and critical constructivist IR, as presented in the previous chapters, are mostly focused on how properties of a system are constituted because it is on this basis that agency is possible.

Nevertheless, as discussed in the previous chapter, if we acknowledge that *people* make politics, it becomes questionable whether a distinction between causation and constitution can be maintained. After all, the horizon is not something that a person can willingly suspend and liberate themselves from. One's trajectory is socially embedded, and because the prejudgements of one's horizon are too, there is a degree of path-orientation – not path-dependence – in how the play of performance may unfold. As I discussed in the previous chapter, ideas and meanings do not float freely because the horizon, whose prejudgements form the constitutive properties, *does* yield a potential causal effect on what is and what is not possible to know. In other words, phronetic and other varieties of knowledge do not fall from the sky and cannot be suspended randomly. Rather, they are socially acquired and held individually.

Based on the insight that some ways of making sense of the world are rather sticky, because sense-making itself is a process and not an instantaneous result of accommodating new information, scholars have begun to acknowledge that a differentiation between causation and constitution is difficult to uphold. Such a differentiation is particularly questionable when developments over time are concerned and when the role of human agency is accounted for as well (Laffey and Weldes 1997; Ruggie 1998; Jackson 2006; Klotz and Lynch 2007; Lebow 2009; Klotz and Prakash 2009; Jackson 2011; Lynch 2014). Questions concern who becomes an actor, how actors are recognised, how identities are sustained, what knowledge is put into what use in plays of performances, and so on. In this regard, it is argued that "[o]ur naïve understanding of cause builds on the concepts of succession and continuity, and the assumption that some necessary connection exists between them" (Lebow 2014: 1). Different to the Wendtian take on the matter, constructivist researchers have argued that constitution and causation may be related and overlapping. If causation is about the "why and how" of physical and social phenomena, and constitution is about "how something is possible and what it is" or "who becomes actors, how they are recognised as such and how they must behave to sustain their identities and status [then] *constitution may work in causal terms*" (Lebow 2009: 213, emphasis added). How a particular course of action becomes possible and how meanings are produced and attached to action, thereby creating interpretive dispositions which open some possibilities for agency but exclude others, is not distinct from causal analysis but rather a part of it (Laffey and Weldes 1997: 205). The resulting analysis is what John Ruggie terms *constitutive causation*, a narrative description of "whatever antecedent conditions, events, or actions are 'significant' in producing or influencing an effect, result, or consequence" (Ruggie 1998: 94).

To be sure, Ned Lebow acknowledges that conflating constitution and cause is "no silver bullet" (Lebow 2009: 215), but providing "causal narratives" (Lebow 2014: 6) allows one to account for ideas and how they play out in processes of embedded agency. In accordance with post-positivist tenets surrounding academic knowledge production, one does not derive a nomothetic explanation (Kratochwil 1993: 66). As Gadamer already held, progress in knowledge in this sense is not *better* understanding but rather a *different* understanding which results from the researcher's broadened horizon. It is presented in the form of a narrative that centres on two aspects. First, it centres on a plot of agency, which includes, for instance, the application of new knowledge based on the fusion of horizons. This aspect considers what happened and how. Second, the focus lies on agency's constitutively causal effect on international relations (Puchala 2003; Neumann 2004; Suganami 2008). This second aspect links the explanation to the broader question of global politics. approaching constitution and causality as related matters for IR scholars who seek to account for the ongoing spinning of a web of meaning through peoples' performances. However, as the focus on constitutive *processes* is

Topoi

One concept that is available, but which has not been comprehensively used in empirical analyses, is that of "topos" (plural: topoi). I introduce it to account for the play of performances in "social imaginaries" (Taylor 2004) through a meta-narrative, thereby acknowledging the double hermeneutic of interpretive research.[4] As it is possible to identify interpretive phases in any research – even positivist research – the explicit development of a narrative improves the transparency of research.[5] My intention is to self-consciously adopt a perspective (Campbell 1992: 4; Löwenheim 2010; Van Milders 2017) that follows from the analysis of the data available. In the remainder of this section, I first introduce a widened understanding of topos which subsumes argumentative social settings in which meanings are (re-)established through linked and differentiated performances. In a second step, I explain that research that takes the double hermeneutic seriously can capture these processes through a meta-narrative that maps these performances. Reconstructing topoi thus takes into account that knowledge is central to world-making. In addition, it is also political because any mapping abstracts from reality and provides a *particular* means of understanding.

As detailed subsequently, the term "topos" derives from narratology and ancient rhetoric. In the context of this book, it refers to an analytical model that explores a space of politics by means of an interpretive analysis of performances (see Table 3.1). At the end of a research project, a topos explains processes with a view to both their empirical part as well as to the theory of international politics.[6] A topos refers to an imagined space that characterises a constellation of meaningful interactions over time. That is, a topos is an abstraction of processes, relations, and interaction that captures politics among people engaged in (re-)forming a world of their making. Topoi are the *plots of plays of performance*. As an adopted perspective, a topos summarises what happened and in what ways a process was meaningful.

Table 3.1 Definition of "topos" and elements of an analysis

Topos	– *Analytical* (not formal) model of politics
	– Abstraction of processes, relations, and interactions
	– Plot of play of performances: what happens and how?
Analysing topoi (double hermeneutic)	– Consider range of communicative forms which contribute to a continuing emergence of meaning
	– Map "play of performances" to derive a meta-narrative

Source: Author

The few occasions on which the term has been presented in constructivist research in IR used the sense of the Aristotelian inventory of rhetoric (Koslowski 1999; Neumann 2001; Bigo and Walker 2007; Kornprobst 2007; Kratochwil 2018), though John Harrington has used the related term "chronotope" in connection with legal practices (Harrington 2018). Friedrich Kratochwil uses the term to denote,

> commonplaces [. . . which not only] establish "starting-points" for arguments, but also locate the issue of a debate in a substantive set of common understandings that provide for the crucial connections within the structure of an argument.
>
> (Kratochwil 1989: 220)

In this understanding, topoi refer to a widely known structure of an argument. The manner in which they are applied is recognisable within a specific context.[7] However, I suggest widening Kratochwil's definition to emphasise the terms "starting point" and "location", because these point us to the indefinite, ever-evolving nature of knowledge: while "starting point" implies the potential for movement and change, "location" establishes the static dimension of knowledge. I argue that it matters to capture both aspects, particularly with a view to making statements about an evolving web of knowledge forming the basis of the normative constitution of global politics.

As discussed in the previous chapter, meaning derives *inter alia* from a series of linkages and differentiations (Hansen 2006: 41f.) which are never fixed and finished. Research on topos/topoi can thus address the *emergence* as well as the *continuing application* of meaning in performances in the hermeneutic sense outlined in the previous chapter. A topos is formed by argumentative interaction based on performances. Expanding Kratochwil's definition given previously, the term "argument" is to be understood not merely as an *utterance* but rather in terms of a broader *social setting*. It might involve contestation, but if we apply a broad understanding of text, this setting is linguistic and non-linguistic and compatible with a spatial understanding of "discourse" (Holzscheiter 2014: 144).[8] Therefore, as expressed in the previous chapter, performances may come in many communicative forms. This broadened understanding of topos helps to capture the full complexity of sense-making that Gadamer referred to as the "universality of language".

As researchers, we have to make sense of these argumentative settings and engage in an open-ended process of map-making. Ludwig Wittgenstein has a spatial understanding of language that is largely compatible with the understanding of performance discussed in the previous chapter and which nicely relates to the spatial implication of topos.[9] It brings us back to the double hermeneutic issue of "making sense of sense-making". He states, "Our language can be regarded as an ancient city: a maze of little streets and squares, of old and new houses, of houses with extensions from various periods, and all this surrounded by a multitude of new suburbs with straight and regular streets and uniform houses" (Wittgenstein 2009 [1953]: para 18).

Topoi are a form of mapping of such an ancient city. Narratology discusses how this can be achieved and in what ways this is a politics practice. Here, the creation of knowledge is a "communicative practice in which someone (a narrator) tells something (a story) to someone (a narratee) about something (a real or imaginary world)" (Kearney 2002: 5 and 150). Richard Kearney, whose roots in hermeneutic philosophy lie with Charles Taylor and Paul Ricœur, summarises the connection between a hermeneutic approach to knowledge and politics as follows:

> It is, in short, only when haphazard happenings are transformed into story, and thus made memorable over time, that we become full agents of our history. This becoming historical involves a transition from the flux of events into a meaningful social or political community.
>
> (Kearney 2002: 3)

While the focus of this book is not on the discussion of concepts of community, it is plain how a topos as an analytical meta-narrative provides a conceptual lens through which analysts can make sense of sense-making processes. Research thus reflexively relates to its object of study because it produces knowledge that might have an influence on how people make politics (Hamati-Ataya 2011; Kornprobst 2013). Mapping plays of performances is political because, by implication, the construction of a meta-narrative in the context of problem-oriented theory-building has to make choices about how constitutive elements are causally related (Klotz and Lynch 2007: 45–51).

A topos maps the play of performances and presents an intelligible account that captures the play's plot. However, in line with hermeneutic reasoning about knowledge discussed in previous chapters, it also underscores that no enquiry starts from scratch. Thus, while much of IR research and discussion of methodology has focused on either "explaining" (deductive) or "understanding" (inductive) modes of enquiry (Hollis and Smith 1990; Keohane 1995 [1989]), the approach presented in this book holds that inductive and deductive movements alternate, making the process of research spiral-like (Bolten 1985). Thus, in fact, *Politics among People* pursues an *abductive* approach which seeks to "make sense" as demanded of a hermeneutic mode of enquiry. Constitutive causation implies that explaining is the primary mode of enquiry, even though this does not mean that one has to subscribe to the nomothetic research tradition.[10]

Every time one seeks to understand a phenomenon, this happens on the basis of one's horizon, which thereby arranges elements and provides an explanation of why things appear as they do. Abduction is different to induction or deduction in that it acknowledges the interpretive situation of the researcher. John Ruggie explains in detail how making sense of events and performances works in terms of deriving a narrative account such as that presented in my discussion of topoi previously. Referring to Donald Polkinghorne's approach to 'emplotment' (1988; 19–20), Ruggie states that,

> The narrative explanatory protocol comprises two "orders" of information: the descriptive and the configurative. The first simply links "events" along a temporal dimension and seeks to identify the effect one has on another.

These events may be more or less "thickly" (i.e., analytically) described (Geertz 1973). Ruggie continues by explaining that,

> The second organizes these descriptive statements into an interpretive "gestalt" or "coherence structure." These gestalt operations rest on a method of interrogative reasoning that Charles Peirce called "abduction:" the successive adjusting of a conjectured ordering scheme to the available facts [involving "a certain element of guess-work," Peirce pointed out], until the conjecture provides as full an account of the facts as possible.
> (Ruggie 1995: 94, referring to Peirce 1955: 151–152)

Ruggie describes two alternating forms of knowledge which are conventionally distinguished as declarative and procedural (compare Anderson 1976). While declarative knowledge captures "facts", such as events, names, and so on, procedural knowledge more closely relates to "fiction", that is, narrative or configurative forms of knowing. This, of course, is the Aristotelian phronetic knowledge discussed in Chapter 1. Both forms of knowledge, the declarative-descriptive as well as the procedural-configurative, matter for this book.

On this basis, the following subsections refine the approach used here. In particular, I begin by discussing criteria of validity in interpretive empirical analyses, which are treated rather quickly by Klotz and Lynch (2007: 20–21) and not at all by others. I then move on to highlight the comparative and sequential nature of interpretive research. Finally, I show how the diligent use of heuristics aids the abductive finding of topoi in the play of performances. As a whole, this section specifies and advances recent methodological discussions in the discipline.

Criteria of validity in interpretive research

The process of finding topoi through problem-based theory-building is advanced by empirical analyses. Conducting empirical analyses is not the exclusive privilege of positivism. Rather, the adjective "empirical" signifies that the process of theory-building is based on data rather than on philosophical reflection. Theory is thus *grounded* in data, which is the basic idea behind a logic of enquiry developed by Barney Glaser and Anselm Strauss in their grounded theory (1967). Consistent with the hermeneutic premise that there is no objective world out there waiting to be discovered, the approach is biased in favour of qualitative research: data does not fall from the sky or simply lie around waiting to be picked up by the researcher. It has to be gathered, which involves a process of selection and interpretation based on the researcher's particular horizon.

As argued in the previous chapter, performances may come in a number of different guises and therefore should be considered during the research process. Data may be retrieved from a variety of sources, including individually held meaning, interaction processes, or the reconstruction of structures and meaningful action (Helfferich 2005; Flick 2009: 29–30). In IR, researchers whose work can be described as sympathetic to hermeneutic approaches have argued to focus on

> Archives of governments, intergovernmental organizations, and non-governmental organizations, letters and memoirs of key individuals, press reports, and interviews, supplemented and contextualized through secondary sources. Treaties, conventions, negotiations, and procedures also manifest actions, such as promising or threatening. [. . . As well as how] people wear clothing, convey meanings that need to be interpreted through non-textual evidence.
>
> (Klotz and Lynch 2007: 19)

Still others have turned to popular culture such as television series or movies (Weldes 1999; Nexon and Neumann 2006), but also to travelogues, literary fiction, ancient poetry, and even opera (Hansen 2006; Lebow 2008, 2012). In the case studies that follow, I focus on interpreting publicly available documents, including the UN Convention on the Law of the Sea and commentaries in professional journals. I also interpret interviews published in books or online and transcripts of speeches or statements. Following Ruggie's quote previously, I link this configurative analysis to the chains of events that mark the trajectory of UNCLOS and the German participation in Kosovo, respectively.

Given such a range of potential and actual sources used in the case studies and the lack of discussion in the broader literature on methodology, questions remain over the validity of interpretations. On the premise that there is no independent standard for assessing the result of research, no Archimedean point through which research can shake the foundations of knowledge (Kratochwil 2007), it is only possible to pit interpretations against each other. That said, certain limitations apply that counter the accusations of relativism and arbitrariness. Some of these narratives are more valid than others and must rely on selection criteria (Klotz and Lynch 2007: 21).

While positivists are interested in the objectivity, reliability, and generalisability of data, that is, the manner in which data resembles "the world out there", I base my analyses of topoi on an alternative set of criteria that have been developed by specialists in qualitative analyses. These criteria are related first to the process of qualitative research and second to the actual practice of interpreting data (Kruse 2011: 266–269).[11] I distinguish three criteria and summarise them in Table 3.2.

A first criterion is that of openness. It is worth remembering that researchers do not stumble across sources but rather generate data themselves. Hence the

Table 3.2 Criteria of validity and consistency

Openness	- Reflexive awareness during process of data collection
	- Leave room for manoeuvring
Intersubjective validation	- Disclose process of data collection
	- Disclose procedure of analysis
	- Validate data within research group (if possible)
Internal consistency	- Topos (outcome) should comprehensively cover all data

Source: Author, based on Kruse (2011)

"quality of qualitative data" (Helfferich 2005) is at stake. As a rule of thumb, states Cornelia Helfferich, data is to be collected in an open-minded and reflexive manner. This means that neither assumptions nor hypotheses nor methods should exclude a change in the direction of research (Mayring 2002: 28). In this manner, qualitative research differs from questionnaire-driven enquiries. A second criterion is intersubjective validation (Kruse 2011: 268), which holds that the standard of validity is not external to data but rather set by the research community. This criterion does not only refer to the output of research (Pouliot 2010: 82) but, once more, also to the process of gathering data. A main feature in this context is the documentation and explication of data *collection* as well as of data *analysis*.

Finally, as a third criterion that ensures the consistency and validity of research, the outcome of data analysis has to live up to the claims it makes. The explaining topos that I produce as a result of my analysis needs to capture the entire material analysed in relation to the original question in an encompassing manner. As it is unlikely that one will discover the topos from a single reading, Pouliot (2010: 85) suggests proceeding until one reaches a point of saturation. That is, one collects data until further fieldwork does not add anything significant to what one has found so far. This suggestion makes sense from a hermeneutic perspective. I suggest calling it "internal consistency", which is meant to describe that research has reached a state of balance in the process of mediating between the general and the particular. Consistent with hermeneutic principles, it should be straightforward to relate a part of the research to the whole and vice versa, bearing in mind that it may be subject to revision at a later point.

Proceeding by comparison and sequence

Adhering to these criteria of validity in the case studies, in order to derive a topos, I proceeded by means of a comparison, particularly (though not exclusively) in terms of an in-case comparison. At the same time, I analysed data sequentially aided by heuristics. It is this theory-guided procedure using comparison and sequence which ultimately accounts for the infinite research process.[12]

With a view to deriving a causally constitutive account of a topos, I explain the three aspects (comparison, sequence, and heuristics) in the following paragraphs, with a particular focus on textual data. Let me begin with clarifying what I mean by comparison. As explained at the beginning of the chapter, in the hermeneutic logic, it becomes difficult to dissect the world into distinct variables. However, following Donatella Della Porta, it is also possible to distinguish between "case-oriented comparisons" and "variable-oriented comparisons" (2008: 202). The aim of case-oriented approaches is to arrive at an in-depth understanding of the research puzzle. She writes,

> small-N, case-oriented comparison usually points at similarities and differences through dense *narratives*, with a large number of characteristics being taken into account, often together with their interaction within long-lasting processes.
> (Della Porta 2008: 204)

What hermeneutic studies thus deal with is a different approach to comparisons than the ones applied in comparative politics and also strands of IR that share the same methodology, that is, a focus on cross-national policy convergence. Case-oriented approaches are studies in which researchers are interested in a particular phenomenon for which the "universe of cases" equals one (or at least not much more than one), because they seek to obtain new and in-depth knowledge about an object (Della Porta 2008: 211ff.).[13]

Hermeneutic approaches are inherently comparative because understanding is only possible by comparing a phenomenon with one's prejudgements. As discussed in Chapters 1 and 2, a general feature of comparison is its contrast with other horizons (Nohl 2009: 54).[14] More conventionally, though, it is a comparison of features within cases that matters more. Here, one delineates the "resources available and [traces] the ways that they are deployed in practice, while sticking close enough to the data that statements about available resources have more of an empirical than a conceptual character" (Jackson 2006b: 266).

Next to comparisons, analyses proceed sequentially. The two aspects are related because dividing texts into sequences allows for a comparison of elements. In particular, researchers may cluster texts around similarities (Nohl 2009: 57), but without looking for regularities and frequency distribution. In this latter line of enquiry, one typically comes across remarks such as "statement X was found in six of the eight interviews". The aim of qualitative research is not the discovery of frequencies (as the sample would be too small anyway) but rather in-depth knowledge of a *gestalt* of a phenomenon (Ruggie 1995; Polkinghorne 2007). Given that understanding requires a fusion of horizons, it should be obvious that a dissection of text into sequences marks a first step in that direction: it is by virtue of relating parts to the whole and the whole to parts that understanding progresses.

During the sequential analysis, I proceed not only comparatively but also in accordance with heuristics derived from theory. As the following table summarises, I suggest dissecting my data along four modes of interaction, with reference to a horizon as well as patterns of action (Table 3.3).[15] It is on the basis of these four modes that I suggest proceeding with analyses of performances, understood as text in general form.

A first manner in which meaning is conveyed is through the interaction process of dialogue. *In a general understanding of text*, this first strand also includes

Table 3.3 Accounting for performance: disclosing meaning

	Text (general)	Text (specific)
1	Interaction: legitimate access	Positioning: role taking
2	Horizon and History I: non-linguistic repertoire of performances	Syntax
3	History and Horizon II: type of performance	Semantics
4	Patterns of action: performances	Gestalt

Source: Author

questions of access, that is, who is considered a legitimate participant in a given dialogue. This consideration matters because it establishes a range of potential conversation partners by positioning them inside or outside a realm of interaction, as discussed in the context of constitutive causality. In a narrower, linguistic sense, the first dimension deals with the dynamics of a conversation. This includes, for instance, references that indicate the taking of roles and which make allusions to self and other in terms of (alleged) competences and the appropriation of rejection thereof. It is part of pragmatic linguistics, which refers to speech acts (Searle 1995), but it also includes what has become known as positioning analysis (for IR, compare Weldes and Saco 1996; Harré and Langenhove 1999). Interpreting a dialogical constellation thus allows me to identify the parties involved and interpret their claim-making with a view to how they thereby (seek to) create worlds of their making. This is part of a process-sensitive understanding of performance as discussed in the previous chapter, in which we cannot necessarily take for granted the existence of a shared background upon which speech acts are possible.[16]

In practice, the first category may overlap in part with the second dimension, which is that of syntax. This category focuses on peculiarities of grammar which cognitive linguistics (Lakoff and Johnson 1980) takes to be a representation of a speaker's horizon. It includes the use of pronouns, negations, passive voice, incomplete sentences, pauses, or the general complexity of speech. As a third category, we can turn to semantic choices that are present in the structures of speech. These include lexical fields, allegories, idioms, and metonyms, as well as the general mode of language use. Cognitive linguistics has emphasised the importance of metaphors that convey one's horizon and which open or foreclose possibilities of action. In IR, scholars have recently begun to systematically make use of metaphor analysis to learn more about the construction of foreign policy relations. They argue that metaphors are specific to a given culture and hence might explain misunderstandings between speakers (Hülsse 2003; Slingerland, Blanchard et al. 2007; Hülsse and Spencer 2008; Spencer 2011). As far as *the more general understanding of text* is concerned, these two distinctions amount to the historical context of performances. Here we deal with the non-linguistic repertoire of performances (Weldes and Saco 1996; Jackson 2006b).[17] This is historically configured and indicative of an actor's horizon, akin to her choice of words and their utterance.

Fourth, in a more *general understanding of text*, one can turn to patterns of action that represent a general order. In linguistic terms, attention is given to narrative figures, that is, the dynamic of organising meaning in a certain plot. This includes addressing how and what is being conveyed, for instance, by determining the use of emotional markers. In combination with the second and third strand, in IR, what has been introduced as predicate analysis (Doty 1993; Milliken 2001) demonstrates how nouns are defined more closely through the use of verbs and attributes. This may allow a speaker to emotionally mark friends and foes and ascribe specific identities to them. As illustrated in Figure 3.1, these instantiations of performance are part of a first descriptive and segmenting step of finding a topos.

54 The topoi of interpretive research

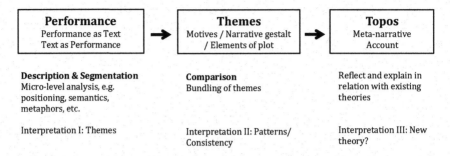

Figure 3.1 From performance to topos

Source: Author, drawn from Kruse (2011: 173 and 186); compare Garfinkel (1967)

Finding topoi

As a way of decelerating the interpretation in a process of comparing and sequential dissection, I suggest using these different guises of plays of performances as theory-derived heuristics for analysing data. They are "thinking tools" (Leander 2008) within the more encompassing thinking tool of "topos". These tools are applied to make qualitative, that is, meaningful, distinctions between sequences of text. They thus allow researchers to make rule-guided discriminations between parts of a performance while adhering to the criterion of intersubjective validation. In combination with the criterion of openness, these tools enlarge or unfold the text. This means that as a part of this enlargement, we slowly begin to develop categories, as indicated in the second step of Figure 3.1 (Kruse 2011: 217–219). These themes resemble containers that are being laden with meaning. This is the part in which the hermeneutic approach differs from content analysis, which defines categories ex ante and applies them to text deductively. Rather, the hermeneutic approach uses categories tentatively for a first attempt at interpreting a section of one's data. Of course, in order to counter accusations that dismiss research in the tradition of grounded theory as relativism and inductive tomfoolery, these interpretations have to be supported by empirical evidence, that is, through references to a performance that is considered typical of the argument one is making (Jackson 2006b: 266).

The following describes how the approach worked in the context of *Politics among People*. After creating these first categories, which may well take more than one round of analysis, I reversed the process of unfolding the text. With a view to getting closer to the goal of devising a topos, in step two (entitled "themes"), categories were put into comparative perspective to one another. The aim was to make the initial interpretation coherent with the data analysed as demanded by the third criterion of validity specified previously. This step prepared the final stage in the research process in which a master category was compared to existing theory.

To summarise the process of research, I began with a development of tentative categories that was facilitated by the different ways in which meaning can be disclosed. The analysis proceeded sequentially because meaning develops over time. Parts of performances were thus identified for comparison and could be grouped into categories. These were meant to be inductive and a tentative reading of my data. The overall process was one in which the original text was unfolded. It was only once I began to bundle categories into "themes" that I developed a more thorough interpretation of performance. Throughout either process, I needed to adhere to criteria of validity and also needed to remain open to being surprised by findings. It was only in the very last step that I developed a final interpretation. It was on this basis that I presented a thematic narrative ("topos") to my audience. Here, I brought my material into comparison with existing theory.

In the following chapters, I present two narratives of different topos: that of "Comtean Positivism", which I argue explains the constitutively causal development of the Law of the Sea, and that of "Humanity", which I hold explains how the German government could participate in NATO missions in former Yugoslavia in the late 1990s, even though the mission was not backed by a UN mandate and despite the coalition parties' tradition of anti-military social movements.

Notes

1 Because researchers hold that their results can be judged as correct or wrong, this approach to science is referred to as foundationalism (Hansen 2011: 169). Foundational science is a feature of a certain theory of knowledge that unfolded through Enlightenment thought. Intended as an objective access to knowledge about the world and an explicit normative intention to better the world by overcoming religious superstition, the approach is referred to as "positivism" by Auguste Comte. Chapter 5 will elaborate on this further as it identifies positivism as the core principle around which the Law of the Sea was established and continues to unfold. For the moment, however, it suffices to say that positivism refers to a general theory of knowledge, while foundationalism is a corresponding epistemological approach.
2 Consider the following example: a stone is a hard object of indeterminate size. While its chemical composition is independent of the meaning it has for a person, it is not inconceivable that a particular stone may be regarded as a weapon for breaking shop windows by one person or take a prominent role in a religious ceremony for another. Hence, the actual performance matters.
3 Usually, this distinction is made with reference to the work of Martin Hollis and Steve Smith (1990).
4 The term meta-narrative is to be used with caution. In the context of this book, it refers to an analytical concept and is limited to a particular context on which the analysis focuses. By contrast, Marx's "historical materialism" can also be regarded as a topos, but the meta-narrative claim in his case is one of an eternal and universal law of history. Still others have recently discovered the analysis of political narratives as a process of sense-making, but without further analytical abstraction or reflection. That is, whereas topos here refers to a meta-narrative that makes sense of sense-making processes, others apply a more literal understanding of narrative that resembles a discussion of ideology.
5 The two phases are discernible at the very beginning of the research process when scholars delineate the universe of their study, including the cases entailed therein,

56 *The topoi of interpretive research*

and towards the end when they have to make sense of the data collected (Puchala 2003: 40f.). Plot charts do not explain themselves, but require a presentation by the researcher.

6   Note that the aim of the book is not to develop a fully fledged theory of IR but rather to derive new insights into concrete phenomena: the UN Convention on the Law of the Sea as well as the German engagement in Kosovo.

7   Three common forms are the topoi of objection, of consequence, and of authority. These refer to different manners in which arguments are exchanged. For instance, the topos of objection is used to reject someone's point of view by claiming that it contradicts either a collectively known premise or a prior statement, while the topos of consequence points out known relations of cause and effect in order to make a statement for one's point of view. In the third instance, topoi of authority are used to criticise someone's statement by referring to singular practices or traits of character of that person that undermine their trustworthiness by suggesting ulterior motives (Lucius-Hoehne and Deppermann 2002: 252).

8   Spatial references have been made elsewhere, and, of course, Pierre Bourdieu's concept of "field" is a case in point. However, as "field" addresses interaction of different forms of capital (e.g. cultural, social, and economic), it does not address processes of understanding (Bourdieu 1983). These matter, though, not least to tell us at what rate different types of capital can be converted.

9   Wittgenstein equates language and Being akin to Gadamer when he writes that "to imagine a language means to imagine a form of life" (2009 [1953]: para 19). Gadamer writes similarly: "Being that can be understood is language" (2004 [1975]: 470, emphasis omitted).

10 Karin Fierke (2005: 14) speaks about abduction but confines this to a discussion of constitution which is, in her view, quite different to causality.

11 Compare Franke and Roos (2017) for similar criteria. This is not the place to compare these approaches, but Kruse's criteria have been tried and tested in a number of research projects over the years. My research benefitted tremendously from his workshops (Hansen-Magnusson 2014).

12 Alexander George and Andrew Bennett emphasise the importance of proceeding in a structured and focused manner; that is, they insist that research should be "structured" by the general questions reflecting the research objective and "focused" by paying attention to some aspects of the case but not others (2005: 68). The outcome of such an enquiry lends itself to comparison across cases.

13 In the terms of positivist research, in-depth analyses sample according to the dependent variable (Della Porta 2008: 212). In IR, there seems to remain a residue of positivist language even among scholars who place themselves outside that camp. For instance, Vincent Pouliot goes into considerable detail to account for the sample of interviewees for his analysis. He writes: "For the Western side I selected a representative sample of countries and organizations. To begin with, I centred on the four core NATO countries whose voices are louder than any other at the North Atlantic Council (NAC) table: the US, the United Kingdom, France and Germany. I also wanted to include less powerful countries, which led me to choose Canada as a representative of smaller founding members, and Poland and Lithuania as newer members of both large and small size" (Pouliot 2010: 84). This procedure is a good example of qualitative sampling, particularly in terms of a theoretically informed *a priori* sample that strives to represent the heterogeneity of the field of study (the alternative being the theoretical sampling advocated by Glaser and Strauss, in which additional cases are added in subsequent rounds of research; see Flick [2009: 158f.]). What is not discussed, though, is the danger that such a sampling approach as applied by Pouliot might replicate false categories (Kruse 2011: 87). It is possible, at least in theory, that criteria other than the ones mentioned matter.

14 For a critical discussion of Nohl's comparative approach, see Kruse (2011: 190f.). Kruse highlights a potential procedural pitfall when comparing publicly available

documents and statements if the researcher intends to overcome the subjective-objective divide. However, for present purposes, this caveat is ignored, as both forms of data are interpreted in a cross-referencing manner rather than sequentially.
15 The approach follows Kruse (Kruse 2011; Kruse, Biesel et al. 2011), who describes a method for analyses of texts in the narrow sense. It integrates several approaches (Lucius-Hoehne and Deppermann 2002; Helfferich 2005; Bohnsack 2008; Nohl 2009) and has been applied in a number of sociological research projects. The account presented here expands his approach by paying closer attention to performance in general terms.
16 For instance, a request such as "please fetch the milk from the fridge" not only establishes a relation between me and the addressee, but also a hierarchy, as I claim to be in a position to make that demand. The addressee, in turn, may accept this constellation and interpret my statement in such a manner that I am pleased with the result. Alternatively, the addressee may reject this relation, for instance, by responding, "Why don't you go and fetch it yourself?"
17 Weldes and Saco (1996) refer to a boycott of embargo as a form of non-linguistic discourse. The closure of naval passages, for instance, may not be verbalised, but it has an effect on others nonetheless.

References

Anderson, J. R. (1976). *Language, Memory, and Thought*. Hillsdale, Erlbaum.
Bernstein, R. J. (1983). *Beyond Objectivism and Relativism: Science, Hermeneutics and Praxis*. Philadelphia, University of Pennsylvania Press.
Bigo, D. and R. Walker (2007). Political Sociology and the Problem of the International. *Millennium – Journal of International Studies* **35**(3): 725–739.
Bohnsack, R. (2008). Rekonstruktive Sozialforschung – Einfuehrung in die Methodologie und Praxis. Opladen, Leske & Budrich.
Bolten, J. (1985). Die hermeneutische Spirale – Überlegungen zu einer integrativen Literaturtheorie. *Poetica* **17**(3/4): 355–371.
Bourdieu, P. (1983, Vol. 2). Ökonomisches Kapital, kulturelles Kapital, Soziales Kapital. *Soziale Ungleichheiten*. R. Kreckel. Göttingen, Verlag Otto Schwarz, Soziale Welt, Sonderband: 183–198.
Campbell, D. (1992). *Writing Security: United States Foreign Policy and the Politics of Identity*. Manchester, Manchester University Press.
Della Porta, D. (2008). Comparative Analysis: Case-Oriented vs. Variable-Oriented Approach. *Approaches and Methodologies in the Social Sciences: A Pluralist Perspective*. D. Della Porta and M. Keating. Cambridge, Cambridge University Press: 198–222.
Doty, R. L. (1993). Foreign Policy as Social Construction: A Post-Positivist Analysis of U. S. Counterinsurgency Policy in the Philippines. *International Studies Quarterly* **37**(3): 297–320.
Fierke, K. (2005). *Diplomatic Interventions – Conflict and Change in a Globalizing World*. Hampshire, Palgrave Macmillan.
Flick, U. (2009). *Qualitative Sozialforschung*. Reinbeck and Hamburg, Rowohlt.
Franke, U. and U. Roos (2017). Rekonstruktive Ansätze in den Internationalen Beziehungen und der Weltpolitikforschung: Objektive Hermeneutik und Grounded Theory. *Handbuch Internationale Beziehungen*. C. Masala and F. Sauer. Wiesbaden, Springer VS: 619–640.
Furlong, P. and D. Marsh (2010). A Skin Not a Sweater: Ontology and Epistemology in Political Science. *Theory and Methods in Political Science*. D. Marsh and G. Stoker. Basingstoke, Palgrave Macmillan: 184–211.
Gadamer, H-G. (2004 [1975]). *Truth and Method*. New York, Continuum.

Garfinkel, H. (1967). *Studies in Ethnomethodology*. Cambridge, Polity Press.
Geertz, C. (1973). *The Interpretation of Cultures: Selected Essays*. New York, Basic Books.
George, A. L. and A. Bennett (2005). *Case Studies and Theory Development in the Social Sciences*. Cambridge, MA and London, The MIT Press.
Glaser, B. G. and A. L. Strauss (1967). *The Discovery of Grounded Theory: Strategies for Qualitative Research*. New York, Aldine de Gruyter.
Haas, P. M. and E. B. Haas (2002). Pragmatic Constructivism and the Study of International Institutions. *Millennium* **31**(3): 573–601.
Hamati-Ataya, I. (2011). The 'Problem of Values' and International Relations Scholarship: From Applied Reflexivity to Reflexivism. *International Studies Review* **13**(2): 259–287.
Hansen, L. (2006). *Security as Practice: Discourse Analysis and the Bosnian War*. London, Routledge.
Hansen, L. (2011). Poststructuralism. *The Globalization of World Politics: An Introduction to International Relations*. J. Baylis, S. Smith and P. Owens. Oxford, Oxford University Press: 166–181.
Hansen-Magnusson, H. (2014). *International Relations as Politics Among People: Towards a Hermeneutic Approach to Global Governance*. Hamburg, Unpubl Dissertation, University of Hamburg.
Harré, R. and L. V. Langenhove (1999). *Positioning Theory: Moral Contexts of Intentional Action*. Oxford, Blackwell.
Harrington, J. (2018). 'We Can't Wait for the Bugs to Spread': Rhetorics of Time, Space and Biosecurity in Global Health Law. *Transnational Legal Theory* **11**(2): 85–109.
Helfferich, C. (2005). *Die Qualität qualitativer Daten – Manual für die Durchführung qualitativer Interviews*. Wiesbaden, VS Verlag für Sozialwissenschaften.
Hollis, M. and S. Smith (1990). *Explaining and Understanding International Relations*. Oxford, Clarendon Press.
Holzscheiter, A. (2014). Between Communicative Interaction and Structures of Signification: Discourse Theory and Analysis in International Relations. *International Studies Perspective* **15**(2): 142–162.
Hülsse, R. (2003). *Metaphern der EU-Erweiterung als Konstruktionen europäischer Identität*. Baden-Baden, Nomos.
Hülsse, R. and A. Spencer (2008). The Metaphor of Terror: Terrorism Studies and the Constructivist Turn. *Security Dialogue* **39**(6): 571–592.
Jackson, P. T. (2006). Making Sense of Making Sense: Configurational Analysis and the Double Hermeneutic. *Interpretation and Method: Empirical Research Methods and the Interpretive Turn*. D. Yanow and P. Schwartz-Shea. Armonk, NY, M. E. Sharpe: 264–280.
Jackson, P. T. (2011). *The Conduct of Inquiry in International Relations: Philosophy of Science and Its Implications for the Study of World Politics*. London and New York, Routledge.
Kearney, R. (2002). *On Stories*. London and New York, Routledge.
Keohane, R. O. (1995 [1989]). International Institutions: Two Approaches. *International Theory. Critical Investigations*. J. Der Derian. New York, New York University Press: 279–308.
King, G., R. O. Keohane and S. Verba (1994). *Designing Social Inquiry – Scientific Inference in Qualitative Research*. Princeton, Princeton University Press.
Klotz, A. and C. Lynch (2007). *Strategies for Research in Constructivist International Relations*. Armonk and London, M. E. Sharpe.
Klotz, A. and D. Prakash, Eds. (2009). *Qualitative Methods in International Relations: A Pluralist Guide*. London, Palgrave Macmillan.

Kornprobst, M. (2007). Argumentation and Compromise: Ireland's Selection of the Territorial Status Quo Norm. *International Organization* **61**(1): 69–98.
Kornprobst, M. (2013). When the Discipline Is Not Enough – Scholarship, Communication, and Power. *Paper Prepared for Presentation at the 8th International Interpretive Policy Analysis Conference (IPA) in Vienna (3–5 July 2013)* [on file with the author].
Koslowski, R. (1999). A Constructivist Approach to Understanding the European Union as a Federal Polity. *Journal of European Public Policy* **6**(4): 561–578.
Kratochwil, F. (1989). *Rules, Norms, and Decisions: On the Conditions of Practical and Legal Reasoning in International Relations and Domestic Affairs*. Cambridge, Cambridge University Press.
Kratochwil, F. (1993). The Embarrassment of Changes: Neorealism as the Science of Realpolitik Without Politics. *Review of International Studies* **19**(1): 63–80.
Kratochwil, F. (2007). Of False Promises and Good Bets: A Plea for a Pragmatic Approach to Theory Building (The Tartu Lecture). *Journal of International Relations and Development* **10**(1): 1–15.
Kratochwil, F. (2018). *Praxis: On Acting and Knowing*. Cambridge, Cambridge University Press.
Kruse, J. (2011). Reader 'Einführung in die Qualitative Interviewforschung'. Freiburg available online: www.qualitative-workshops.de.
Kruse, J., K. Biesel and C. Schmieder (2011). *Metaphernanalyse: Ein rekonstruktiver Ansatz*. Wiesbaden, VS Verlag für Sozialwissenschaften.
Laffey, M. and J. Weldes (1997). Beyond Belief: Ideas and Symbolic Technologies in the Study of International Relations. *European Journal of International Relations* **3**: 193–237.
Lakoff, G. and M. Johnson (1980). *Metaphors We Live By*. Chicago and London, University of Chicago Press.
Leander, A. (2008). Thinking Tools: Analyzing Symbolic Power and Violence. *Qualitative Methods in International Relations: A Pluralist Guide*. A. Klotz and D. Prakash. Basingstoke, Palgrave Macmillan.
Lebow, R. N. (2008). *A Cultural Theory of International Relations*. Cambridge, Cambridge University Press.
Lebow, R. N. (2009). Constitutive Causality: Imagined Spaces and Political Practices. *Millennium – Journal of International Relations* **38**(2): 211–239.
Lebow, R. N. (2012). *The Politics and Ethics of Identity*. Cambridge, Cambridge University Press.
Lebow, R. N. (2014). *Constructing Cause in International Relations*. New York, Cambridge University Press.
Löwenheim, O. (2010). The 'I' in IR: An Autoethnographic Account. *Review of International Studies* **36**(4): 1023–1045.
Lucius-Hoehne, G. and A. Deppermann (2002). *Rekonstruktion narrativer Identität: Ein Arbeitsbuch zur Analyse narrativer Interviews*. Opladen, Leske und Budrich.
Lynch, C. (2014). *Interpreting International Relations*. New York and London, Routledge.
Mayring, P. (2002). *Qualitative Sozialforschung*. Weinheim and Basel, Beltz.
Milliken, J. (2001). *Discourse Study: Bringing Rigor to Critical Theory*. Armonk and London, M. E. Sharpe: 136–160.
Neumann, I. B. (2001). The English School and the Practices of World Society. *Review of International Studies* **27**(3): 503–507.
Neumann, I. B. (2004). Beware of Organicism: The Narrative Self of the State. *Review of International Studies* **30**(2): 259–267.

Nexon, D. and I. Neumann, Eds. (2006). *Harry Potter and International Relations*. Lanham, Rowman & Littlefield.

Nohl, A-M. (2009). *Interview und dokumentarische Methode: Anleitungen für die Forschungspraxis*. Wiesbaden, VS Verlag für Sozialwissenschaften.

Peirce, C. S. (1955). *Philosophical writings of Peirce*. New York, Dover Publications.

Polkinghorne, D. (1988). *Narrative Knowing and the Human Sciences*. Albany, NY, State University of New York Press.

Polkinghorne, D. (2007). Validity Issues in Narrative Research. *Qualitative Inquiry* **13**(4): 471–486.

Pouliot, V. (2010). *International Security in Practice: The Politics of NATO-Russia Diplomacy*. Cambridge, Cambridge University Press.

Puchala, D. (2003). *Theory and History in International Relations*. New York and London, Routledge.

Ruggie, J. G. (1995). Peace in Our Time? Causality, Social Facts and Narrative Knowing. *Proceedings of the Annual Meeting (American Society of International Law)* **89**: 93–100.

Ruggie, J. G. (1998). *Constructing the World Polity: Essays on International Institutionalization*. London and New York, Routledge.

Searle, J. R. (1995). *The Construction of Social Reality*. London, Penguin.

Slingerland, E., E. M. Blanchard and L. Boyd-Judson (2007). Collision with China: Conceptual Metaphor Analysis, Somatic Marking, and the EP-3 Incident. *International Studies Quarterly* **51**(1): 53–77.

Spencer, A. (2011). Bild Dir Deine Meinung: Die metaphorische Konstruktion des Terrorismus in den Medien. *Zeitschrift für Internationale Beziehungen* **18**(1): 47–76.

Suganami, H. (2008). Narrative Explanation and International Relations: Back to Basics. *Millennium – Journal of International Relations* **37**(2): 327–356.

Taylor, C. (2004). *Modern Social Imaginaries*. London and Durham, Duke University Press.

Van Milders, L. (2017). Interpretation, Judgement, and Dialogue: Reclaiming Causation in Critical Terrorism Studies. *Critical Studies on Terrorism* **10**(2): 220–239.

Wæver, O. (1996). The Rise and Fall of the Inter-Paradigm Debate. *International Theory: Positivism & Beyond*. S. Smith, K. Booth and M. Zalewski. Cambridge, Cambridge University Press: 149–185.

Waltz, K. N. (1979). *Theory of International Politics*. New York, McGraw-Hill.

Weldes, J. (1999). Going Cultural: Star Trek, State Action, and Popular Culture. *Millennium – Journal of International Studies* **28**(1): 117–134.

Weldes, J. and D. Saco (1996). Making State Action Possible: The United States and the Discursive Construction of 'The Cuban Problem', 1960–1994. *Millennium: Journal of International Studies* **25**(2): 361–395.

Wendt, A. (1998). On Constitution and Causation in International Relations. *Review of International Studies* **24**(5): 101–117.

Wittgenstein, L. (2009 [1953]). *Philosophische Untersuchungen/Philosophical Investigations*. Oxford, B. Blackwell.

4 The UN Convention on the Law of the Sea

The case: bringing UNCLOS as politics among people to IR

This chapter and the next illustrate the insights that an approach centred on "politics among people" holds for IR. Both chapters feature cases that are of continuing importance for understanding the normative composition of contemporary global politics. This chapter primarily interprets the structural evolution of the Law of the Sea, while the next chapter focuses on meanings and interpretations of people in particular situations. I argue that a focus on "politics among people" makes the long-term impact that the cases have on international relations comprehensible because the approach focuses on human agency and the continuous spinning of a web of meaning through performances.

In this chapter, I analyse the United Nations Convention on the Law of the Sea (UNCLOS). The core questions are: which play of performance brings UNCLOS about, and what is the topos that explains its trajectory? I therefore follow Philip Steinberg's call to look at the ocean holistically in terms of the processes that shape human interaction in a particular space and how that space is, in turn, shaped by humans (2001: 10). Historically, oceans were theorised in a recurring dispute over open vs. closed waters and the ensuing regime of sovereignty. Disputes centred on Hugo Grotius's arguments put forward in support of the Dutch East India Company for open waters (*mare liberum*) and the argumentation by John Selden, according to whom nations with a longer sea-faring tradition such as England, Spain, and Portugal should legitimately control access to the sea (*mare clausum*). With a view to enabling a debate over the significance of contemporary Law of the Sea, I argue that its emergence and continuing relevance become understandable through the topos of "Comtean Positivism", which comprises elements of objectivity, humanity, and expertocracy. Following the method discussed in the previous chapter, the topos was abductively reconstructed from publicly available sources, including interview statements, speeches, documents, legal commentary, and narrative accounts of participants at the convention negotiation.[1] It allows me to conclude that the Law of the Sea is characterised by an increasing reliance on methods of natural sciences and expertocracy. The role of science and scientists as experts in core areas of UNCLOS, and its practical instantiation, de-politicises the ways in which the Law of the Sea works. This development makes it difficult, perhaps impossible, to ensure the original intention behind the codification of the Law of the Sea, that is, the seas' use and preservation for humankind.

UNCLOS is a key part of contemporary ocean governance and hence of the Law of the Sea.[2] Given that it has been referred to as a constitution for the oceans (Koh 1983: xxxiii), its existence presents a puzzle to IR scholars. I argue that UNCLOS should be approached as politics among people in order to make sense of the play of performances that (re-)instantiate the convention on an ongoing basis, because doing so allows researchers to see more than the formal organisational structure, which comprises the International Tribunal for the Law of the Sea (ITLOS), the International Seabed Authority (ISA), and the Committee on the Limits of the Continental Shelf (CLCS). Approaching the Law of the Sea as politics among people explains its historical trajectory as well as its ongoing development and also paves the way for an encompassing analysis of recent political events, including the display of a Russian flag at the North Pole (Dodds 2010)[3] and Danish and Canadian claims to parts of the Arctic (Wood-Donnelly 2019)[4] as well as Chinese and Japanese claims to sovereignty over the Diaoyu/Senkaku islands.[5]

Although UNCLOS was agreed upon in 1982 and entered into force in 1994, it has received little attention in IR compared to the mushrooming discussion in international law.[6] Its character of a "constitution", however, poses questions to those areas of IR theory that consider global politics a rule-free world of anarchy (Waltz 1979). Furthermore, as far as the ocean floor and especially the Arctic are concerned, the enormous anticipated costs of developing these areas for mining, oil drilling, or waterways do not provide a rational incentive to maximise profits from exploitation (Keohane 1984; critically Egede 2004; Keil 2014). The few times that IR scholars have engaged with the development of the Law of the Sea have been in the context of regime analyses and economic relations beyond rational means-end calculations (Haas 1975; Haas 1980; Wolf 1991). Rather than starting the enquiry from assumptions about fixed state preferences or identities, a focus on the performances and horizons seems more fruitful to shed light on how ocean governance works in practice.

By contrast, in international law, the discussion is alive and more recent. Scholars present during the convention provide detail-rich discussions of the development as well as specific legal issues and the organisation of the Law of the Sea, such as the accounts by Stevenson and Oxman as well as more recent discussions (Stevenson and Oxman 1974, 1975; Oxman 1977, 1978, 1979, 1980; Buzan 1981; Oxman 1981, 1982, 1995, 1996; Suarez 2008; Rothwell and Stephens 2010; Harrison 2011). Only a few scholars provide an account of the Law of the Sea with a view towards a normative political debate (Byers 2009). If we accept the view that the Law of the Sea is alive and continuously evolving through processes of interpretation and practice (Higgins 1995; Klabbers 2006, with particular regard to the Law of the Sea, see Nordquist, Norton Moore et al. 2013), the fact that UNCLOS is referred to as a constitution for the oceans (Koh 1983: xxxiii) *should* attract the attention of IR scholars. I argue that fundamental questions of politics, such as who gets what, when, and how (Lasswell 1990), need to be addressed in light of the recent activities outlined previously. It is apparent that the oceans' constitution

The UN Convention on the Law of the Sea 63

has not settled but rather marks the beginning of a debate (Klabbers 2006: 295). Given that IR has all but ignored what happened on the oceans in the past decades but might be forced to deal with ocean governance in the near future (Barkin and DeSombre 2013; Webster 2015; Tiller and Nyman 2018), I hold that a better understanding of the trajectory of the Law of the Sea from an IR perspective is *necessary*,[7] and it is *possible* based on an approach built on politics among people.

The remainder of the chapter first outlines the study in terms of the data used and the process of analysis. Based on the discussion in the previous chapter, I specifically refer to UNCLOS Article 76, as it occupies a central position in the contemporary debate. Following the outline of the study, the chapter continues with a brief discussion of Auguste Comte's positivism, which I take to be the central trait of the topos of the Law of the Sea. This section highlights the central themes of Comte's social theory, which are subsequently illustrated with references to the continuous re-making of the Law of the Sea. To reiterate, I do not apply Comte deductively to the case but rather choose to begin with the conclusion to make it easier for readers to follow the argument. I conclude with a discussion of how contemporary maritime governance should be a case of politics among people, in which access to an open debate is hindered by depoliticising key decisions of legal and scientific experts.

Outline of the case study: data and the process of analysis

What is at stake in contemporary ocean governance, and how can IR make sense of it? As a precursor to understanding the ongoing development of the Law of the Sea and its relevance to ocean governance, the study presented in this chapter centres on the topos of "Comtean Positivism", which I reconstruct from data drawn from a range of textual sources. The enquiry aims to explain the play of performances regarding the Law of the Sea as a result of politics among people and the hermeneutic encounters between them. This chapter differs from the following one in that it focuses on horizons as well as the general "grammar" of performances, in particular the codification of UNCLOS as well as its trajectory since. Which kind of performances can explain the trajectory of UNCLOS, and what conclusions can be drawn regarding the normative constitution of contemporary ocean governance? I argue that the core features of Comte's positivism, namely humanity, objectivity, and expertocracy, help us in answering this question.

This section explicates the underlying assumptions of the study. It thereby speaks to the criteria of validity discussed in Chapter 3, making transparent the sources of data and the heuristics used for the analysis, as well as the conclusions that can be drawn from the study.

Data from which the topos is reconstructed can be found from a range of publicly available sources. They include, for instance, specialised journals, but of course these have to be handled with the appropriate amount of care as required with any use of sources.[8] Participants in the convention annually summarised what they considered the main trends of the negotiations in the *American Journal of International Law,* and more recent developments are covered in *Ocean*

Development and International Law. Other, more immediate statements by people involved in shaping UNCLOS that did not pass through review processes are rare, the famous exception being Arvid Pardo's speech at the UN General Assembly in 1967 and more recent speeches in commemoration of the event by close friends and colleagues of his, which are retrievable online. Clyde Sanger (1986) has compiled a book that contains interview excerpts and anecdotal descriptions of how different aspects of the convention were formulated. In order to trace, interpret, and reconstruct the development of knowledge resources, I treat these sources as if they contained data collected in interviews conducted by myself. Alongside the accounts of the conference published in law journals, they provide interpretable empirical material related to open-ended performances.

I contextualise the statements by joining them with background information which I obtained from interviews with Renate Platzöder, who played a pivotal role in documenting the convention and its aftermath, and Karl Hinz, who served as a member on the Commission on the Limits of the Continental Shelf. Further information was obtained from rulings by the International Court of Justice (ICJ). In methodological terms, I treat these rulings as quasi-settled social facts on the basis of which speech acts are possible.[9] They form heuristics for the interpretation process. This careful use of law is warranted, I argue, given that the convention proceeded without the usual extensive preparation of legal documents by the International Law Commission of the United Nations (Manley 1979: 11–12; Larson, Roth et al. 1995: 288–289). Thus the convention captures a spectrum of performances in which the room to manoeuvre for the actors differs: while the agreement to proceed by consensus under the so-called "gentlemen's agreement" (Haas 1975; Eustis 1977: 234; Buzan 1981),[10] which was ratified by the UN General Assembly on 16 November 1973, and the waiving of extensive preparatory documentation created space for open trajectories, it is reasonable to assume that most participants were familiar with past codifications of the Law of the Sea, as well as its customs. I consider this familiarity to be part of participants' phronetic background knowledge and to play a causally constitutive role in the trajectory of the development of UNCLOS.

The case study has two aims. With the first, I seek to advance the theoretical and methodological discussion of constructivism in IR, as discussed in Chapters 2 and 3. The case is used for illustrating purposes of how international politics can be approached as politics among people. To this end, I show how performances unfold and constitutively cause the Law of the Sea. Indicators of this process are, for instance, intertextual links across different sets of data – not only references in documents but also in statements by people involved or in court rulings. As the second aim, the study makes a contribution to the analysis of contemporary ocean governance. The topos reconstructed in this chapter is an exercise in problem-oriented theory-building. To achieve this aim, I use the indicators interpretively in the manner outlined in the previous chapter. I search for an emerging theme and general characteristic features, from which I derive a topos that represents a full account of my analysis, after reiterated sequential analyses and comparisons across different pieces of data. This approach is in line with the criteria of validity discussed in the previous chapter.

Comte's positivism

I argue that the topos of "Comtean Positivism" holds strong explanatory power regarding the emergence of the codified Law of the Sea, as well as its ongoing institutionalisation in UNCLOS. The topos helps us to theorise the state of contemporary ocean governance because Comte discusses processes centring on knowledge and knowledge creation, and his concepts are embedded in a normative social theory. His "positivism" includes more than "empiricism", the current understanding in academia (Wagner 2001: 37), and rests on the three principles of objectivity, humanity, and expertocracy. I concluded during the latter stages of the interpretation of my data, when I began bundling themes and subjecting them to comparison, that this topos is more suitable for explaining contemporary ocean governance than potential alternatives that could have been derived from other available social theories. Comte's positivism does not solely focus on material, particularly the economic aspects that form the core of Marxist social theories, nor does it neglect human agency, as do system-oriented theories.[11] The elements of Comte's positivism explain the development *and* continuing play of performances through which the Law of the Sea is recreated on a daily basis.

As I do not assume readers are overly familiar with the work of Comte, I contextualise his theory and explain the main components of the topos before I present the findings in the next section.

The context in which Comte developed his theory was marked by a secularisation of French society in which monarchy gave way to a republic, followed by Jacobite despotism and a counter-revolution after which Napoleon ascended as a quasi-monarchic head of state. Enlightenment ideas resonated among the middle classes, who increasingly questioned traditional forms of authority derived from religious ideals. This included the God-given legitimacy of monarchy, but also the religious calendar that structured the year. The bourgeoisie-turned-citizens set out to replace the head of state, quite literally, as well as the calendar. However, even the new constitution did not pacify society until Napoleon replaced the republic with military despotism, and the revolutionary calendar with the old Gregorian one, on 1 January 1806 (Wagner 2001: 14–18).

Throughout Comte's lifetime, these tensions proved influential to his work. Building on the teachings of Henri de Saint Simon but also amending and moving beyond these (Bernart 2003: 31–33), at the centre of Comte's writings is a theory of society which identifies two simultaneous yet contrary developments. Asserting the declining role of religion and contrasting this development with a heightened importance of natural sciences (Gane 2006: 2 and 93f.), Comte presents a three-stage model of social progression throughout history, a motif that he shares with contemporary social theorists and utopians of the nineteenth century such as Karl Marx. Other than Marx, though, who focused on industrial forces of production and hence factors internal to a given society, the driving forces in Comte's model in the last of the three stages are the natural sciences. They share in common that they operate according to mathematical principles; that is, they seek to establish laws which describe distinct relations between component parts existing within their respective realm of study. In this light, Comte identifies a successive development that began with mathematics and was followed by astronomy, physics, chemistry, and biology, which all struggled to overcome theology as a source of explanation. In Comte's view, writes Mike Gane, nature "is in many ways capable of being modified to the benefit of Humanity" (2006: 92). Drawing on the same methodology as the natural sciences, Comte argues that the time is ripe to engage with what he initially referred to as "social physics" before coining the term "sociology" in 1838 (Bernart 2003: 36).

With this in mind, it becomes clear that Comte's analysis is not just a philosophical exercise but actually contains a normative political programme. The aim of his social theory is to overcome the clash between aristocratic-religious restoration, on the one hand, and the democratic-anarchic sovereignty of the people, on the other, both of which marked the decades before and after the revolution of 1789. Instead, Comte is interested in devising a social order that is in accordance with the idea of human betterment and progress through the course of history and which would stand the test of time (Wagner 2001: 7). The teleological development that Comte asserts is a utopian vision in which the fate of humankind is positive. Hence, "positivism" becomes the label of his overall theory.

The appropriate solution, in his view, rests in a new religion of reason that is devoid of metaphysics. Instead, its focus should rest on humanité/humanity (Wagner 2001: 64–65), cultivating a set of rituals that were modelled after Catholic forms of worship.[12] Comte's idea of the "Occidental Republic", in which such a cult of humanity was to be realised, surpasses the boundaries of the French state and explicitly includes all peoples of Europe and potentially a world society which was supposed to model itself after the European bourgeoisie.

For Comte, the fulfilment of the Occidental Republic lies in establishing a sociocracy, defined as the government of society (Wagner 2001) or sociologists (Gane 2006: 7).[13] This polity marks the new age of positivism and is supposed to rest on an alliance between the proletariat, women, and scientists.[14] It is marked by a hierarchical order in which the scientists rule for the benefit of all (Rolshausen 2001: 89), because each contributor does what he or she does best (Wagner 2001: 35). While the proletariat works and women provide emotional support, Comte argues, scientists assume a particularly important role because they are able to deal with societal problems in an objective manner (Gane 2006: 3). They are therefore, in Comte's view, particularly qualified to control the fate of society. In accordance with the idea that society progresses over time, objectivity is a quality that sets scientists apart from the theologians of the religious phase. In Comte's view, objectivity applied for the benefit of humankind is also a quality that was lacking in both the aristocracy and the bourgeoisie before and after the French Revolution. Hence, scientists must take the lead in all social affairs – a vision of society that is modelled after the spiritual priesthood found in Catholic hierarchies (ibid. 5). As far as matters of nature are concerned, astronomers, biologists, and so on are experts over their object of study. In Comte's view, sociologists, in drawing on the epistemological tools of the natural sciences, are able to recognise social patterns and apply their insights to governance mechanisms for the benefit of society at large (Rolshausen 2001: 90).

The three elements of the topos of "Comtean Positivism" – objectivity, humanity, and expertocracy – fulfil different roles in his theory but are closely related. Objectivity is the guiding principle for action, alleging that subjectivity and metaphysics distort one's view of what actually *is* and thereby cloud judgement of what one should do. Expertocracy is the obvious way to organise decision-making, emphasising the role of knowledge and knowledge creation and the alleged rationalism that is associated with knowing (as opposed to feeling). As an aside, the recent field of what is termed science diplomacy clearly builds on this narrative of the superiority of knowledge and expertise for international politics (Berkman, Kullerud et al. 2017). Finally, humanity designates who stands to benefit from the politics that "Comtean Positivism" purports to bring.

Based on these three core features of "Comtean Positivism", I will present the topos with regard to UNCLOS in the following section. As summarised in the following table (Table 4.1), each section will specify the respective horizon and the stock of knowledge which was conducive to creating the convention text in plays of performances. The three core features of Comte's positivism continue to matter for the instantation of UNCLOS today.

Humanity: making the Law of the Sea

In the opening paragraph of this chapter, I alluded to the recurring dispute over open vs. closed waters and the ensuing regime of sovereignty. As we will see

Table 4.1 Fusing horizons to (re-)create UNCLOS

Horizon/prejudice		"Common heritage of humankind"; informal text and negotiations ↓	Cases of international law; Conventions I (1930) and II (1960) ↓	Existing territorial zones; concept of "natural prolongation" ↓
Topos of "Comtean Positivism" characteristic of UNCLOS III	Transformed during 1973–1982 and valid today	Humanity	Expertocracy	Objectivity
		Open-ended and informal consultation process	Organisational setting: ITLOS, ISA, CLCS	Standardised procedures, e.g. Article 76 delimiting the continental shelf (natural sciences fused with law)

Source: Author

subsequently, the tension between open and closed waters continues today, though in practice the oceans have become ever more governed, and thereby closed, through national and international jurisdiction. However, prior to the negotiation of the Law of the Sea convention, in Arvid Pardo's appeal to the "common heritage of mankind" [sic], it is possible to discern an approach that seeks to overcome this division. This is similar to Comte's notion of humanity, which contains an appeal to humanity as a principle transcending particularisms. As a core component of the topos, humanity matters in two respects: the content of the Law of the Sea, and the manner in which it came about.

Concerning the content of the convention, Pardo's idea is arguably the most prominent performance in this aspect of contemporary Law of the Sea. Its origins lie within a broader ecological movement, and it was particularly developed in close relation with Elizabeth Mann-Borghese (Baker 2011).[15] As explained by Pardo, the common heritage is deemed worthy of protection because it is supposed to belong to everyone and no one in particular. Humankind, in Pardo's rather melodramatic introduction, can be regarded as possessing a deep ontological bond with all matters of the ocean. Paragraph 7 of his speech makes this clear:

> The dark oceans were the womb of life: from the protecting oceans life emerged. We still bear in our bodies – in our blood, in the salty bitterness of our tears – the marks of this remote past. Retracing the past, man [sic], the present dominator of the emerged earth, is now returning to the ocean depths.
> (Pardo 1967: para 7)

Given that life emerged from the oceans, it is plausible that maritime affairs deserve special attention. Pardo accordingly phrases the recent developments as a matter of life or death:

> His [sic] penetration of the deep could mark the beginning of the end for man, and indeed for life as we know it on this earth: it could also be a unique opportunity to lay solid foundations for a peaceful and increasingly prosperous future for all peoples.
> (ibid.)

Pardo's conclusion was that the Law of the Sea of the time was ill equipped to keep pace with technological advances that would allow exploitation of resources as well as increased military use. In his view, this would inevitably result in national appropriation of what he considered the "common heritage of mankind" (ibid. para 13) and would also carry the danger of being polluted through nuclear waste.[16]

Pardo's speech was given at a time of decolonisation when newly independent states demanded access to the oceans. At the same time, industrialised countries were seeking a way to harvest manganese nodules from the ocean floor, which contain traces of a number of chemical elements used to purify processed metal. Emphasising the united fate of humanity, his concept entailed a new form of sovereignty that held a largely functional rather than a national outlook. Functional sovereignty envisaged that resources would be exploited in a new system of management that would ensure a (partial) redistribution of benefits around the globe, while jurisdiction would be granted for certain uses rather than entire geographical spaces (Wolf 1981: 59; Suarez 2008: 39).

The second manner in which performing humanity mattered concerns the conduct of the negotiations that brought UNCLOS about. In addition to the gentlemen's agreement mentioned at the beginning of this chapter, the negotiation was driven by informal proceedings. The proceedings of the third Law of the Sea conference (UNCLOS III) centred on a process of text writing in which the text was considered an "informal negotiating text" rather than a "negotiated" text – suggesting that it continued to be open to discussion and re-writing. It has been identified as an "active consensus procedure" (Buzan 1981: 334), aiming to include all participants. At the same time, informal sessions served to expand or alter the common understanding of the status quo – making the negotiation into an encounter between people rather than between delegates of states. Proceeding informally was a conscious decision of the group based on the experience of the difficult discussion of the "major trends" report to the UN General Assembly after the Caracas session of 1974. Sanger quotes Rapporteur-General Ken Rattray:

> [W]e took a decision that there would be no further reports [to the General Assembly] lest it might harden positions which had been taken. Therefore we decided to hold [a number of] meetings in informal plenary or informal committee without records, so that people can speak more freely in the hope of groping to find solutions [. . .] it was essential, if we were to get consensus, because once people go on the record in stating positions it becomes increasingly difficult for them to reverse themselves.
>
> (Sanger 1986: 43)

If we enquire into how it was possible to advance the convention text in several stages, of which none was considered to present a formalised version, we need to take a close look at the working arrangement. Central to the progress of the text through different stages was an informal working arrangement adopted by the so-called Evensen group, named after its chairman Jens Evensen of Norway. Evensen personally invited members of this group by letter. In accordance with the theme of humanity and inclusion, they were asked to join as individuals and not as members of their national delegation. Evensen recalls,

> [When we met] we were putting aside our nationality and our status as heads of delegations. It was always an anonymous document we produced. I would try to draft the essence of our discussions and send it round the group. We had never any kind of decision machinery: we didn't vote or do anything. I wrote drafts and we discussed them, and I had to go back and write something else, more or less what was floating in the air. This could happen three or four times. Then, if the others didn't protest too vigorously, we wrote a final

paper – for example, on the continental shelf, the economic zone, or questions of pollution and scientific research and so on.

I gave these papers as anonymous documents from "Friends of the President" to Shirley Amerasinghe [the conference president, HHM] and he included them in his first negotiating text. A great number of chapters were worked out in this way.

(Sanger 1986: 29–30)

Sergio Thompson-Flores, a regular member of the Evensen group, recounts,

[T]he Evensen Group played a very important part. It launched the system that was adopted by the whole conference. [. . .] Each one expressed his own point of view and Evensen then drafted his middle-of-the road provisions that he thought might be acceptable to the majority. It was a very *curious exercise, seldom used in international negotiations – but it was so useful that the Conference* adopted it as its way of operating. So the Evensen Group in one sense expanded into the full conference.

(Sanger 1986: 30)

Remarkably, the idea of an informal group had not been devised by Evensen himself. Rather, he had been approached by Jack Stevenson of the United States and Alexander Yankov of Bulgaria – an unusual constellation in itself, given the prevailing confrontation between the United States and the Soviet Bloc – who were convinced that the negotiations would not lead anywhere without a drafting group (Sanger 1986: 29). The group developed a close rapport, which can be regarded as a shared horizon, and a firm commitment to advance the negotiations. Evensen even invited participants to Geneva for an informal, intersessional meeting in early 1977 (Oxman 1978: 57).

As it turned out, the hermeneutic encounters of the inclusive procedure made it possible to overcome a widespread scepticism about the conference's success that prevailed among commentators during the early sessions. Commentators feared that because the number of participating countries had surpassed 150 since the process of decolonisation, actors from diverse backgrounds would come into contact and make a consensus implausible (Stevenson and Oxman 1974; Eustis 1977). As if to prove the sceptics wrong, however, allegiances formed not necessarily only in the predictable patterns, that is, in clusters of industrialised countries with broad coastlines, landlocked and geographically disadvantaged states, the Soviet Union and Eastern European countries, and so on, but also in unexpected constellations, that is, between industrialised and developing countries.[17] The inclusive principle of humanity made it possible to advance the text through different stages to arrive at a convention text in 1982.

Objectivity: delimiting the continental shelf

What about the Comtean theme of objectivity? Next to the understanding that states can have legitimate claims to the ocean – which was already at the heart of the controversy in Grotius's times – the most important prejudgement in delegates' horizons was probably the idea that somehow the ocean floor formed a natural prolongation of the land. "Objectivity" thus became central to making the Convention, and has remained so until the present.

The groundwork for this notion was laid over a couple of decades prior to the negotiations. Following the end of WWII and 15 years after a failed conference in The Hague in 1930, US President Truman declared that US territory would extend beyond the conventional 3-mile zone, now comprising what his declaration identified as the "continental shelf". Without setting an explicit delimitation in terms of nautical miles, what is now known as the Truman Proclamation stated that natural resources as well as fish stocks belonged to the United States – up to a depth of 100 fathoms, that is, 200 metres. More specifically, highlighting a number of ways in which activities on land or geological features stretch beyond the shore, on 28 September 1945, US President Truman proclaimed that,

> the exercise of jurisdiction over the natural resources of the subsoil and sea bed of the continental shelf by the contiguous nation is reasonable and just, since the effectiveness of measures to utilize or conserve these resources would be contingent upon cooperation and protection from the shore, since the continental shelf may be regarded as an extension of the land-mass of the coastal nation and thus naturally appurtenant to it, since these resources frequently form a seaward extension of a pool or deposit lying within the territory, and since self-protection compels the coastal nation to keep close watch over activities off its shores which are of the nature necessary for utilization of these resources.[18]

Next to the general declaration of taking possession of maritime resources, the noteworthy passage is the non-specific manner in which the statement is framed. No reference is made as to the extent of the continental shelf other than it being "naturally appurtenant" to the nation's land mass. In a commentary on this proclamation, Klaus Dieter Wolf regards this as a shift in emphasis away from trade or fishery interests towards securing off-shore oil and gas (Wolf 1981: 48), which might have been accelerated by a general post-WWII scarcity of resources (see Suarez 2008: 27).

Regardless of what might have been the true intentions behind the proclamation, the US claim ignited a wave of similar unilateral declarations over the coming decade and helped to establish the notion that there were objectively discernible demarcations in the oceans. Particularly, South American states began to claim ownership over a zone of 200 nautical miles off their coasts in order to limit foreign access to fishing grounds.[19] As nations along the West coast of South America do not have a comparable continental shelf, it made no sense to follow the US example directly. However, the United States only laid claim to particular resources and did not refer to the water column and the air space above; Chile, Peru, and Ecuador included this extension in their declarations (Wolf 1981: 48; Heidar 2004: 21f.). This did not pass uncontested, as it led commentators at the time to fear that the concept of *mare liberum* would increasingly be replaced by

72 *The UN Convention on the Law of the Sea*

mare clausum approaches (Friedmann 1973: 763). However, the extension eventually prevailed and proved influential for the subsequent understanding of the Law of the Sea as expressed in Article 76.[20]

Article 76 is a perfect example of how the notion of objectivity is embedded in the Convention. For the most part, Article 76 clarifies that the limit of the territorial sea is 200 nautical miles (nm) in cases where the continental shelf is less than 200 nm in width and expands on the exception (Art. 76.1). The first part of the Article refers to geological-sounding concepts such as "continental slope" and "continental rise". It makes the ocean floor seem a feature-rich area in which different formations can be distinguished. In practice, however, this is far more complicated. Paragraph 76.4 sets out to specify two ways in which the outer edge of the continental margin is to be established. Both approaches centre on identifying what geologists have termed the "foot" of the continental slope, defined as the "point of maximum change in the gradient" at the base of the slope [Article 76.4 (b)]. Once the foot of the slope is identified, the first option comprises determining the points where the thickness of sedimentary rock is at least 1% of the shortest distance to the foot of the slope [see 76.4 (a – i)]. A thickness of 1 mile would thus enable a state to place a coordinate at 100 miles outside the foot of the continental slope. Alternatively, 76.4 (a-ii) identifies the option that states pick points not more than 60 nm outside the foot of the continental slope.

Critical commentators explain that the horizon of the drafters of UNCLOS must have a particular image of what a continental margin looks like. The two options, in which the margin either lies within the 200-nm limit or exceeds it and thus triggers measurement activity, can be graphically represented as in Figure 4.1.

However, the actual issue of contention and resulting ambiguity is that in reality the continental shelf and margin rarely correspond to the form illustrated in the diagram. Few participants at the UNCLOS negotiations seem to have been aware of this fact, as most geological research on this matter was undertaken in the years following the convention. Nowadays, scientists

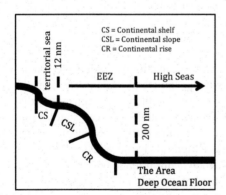 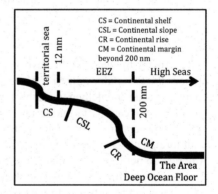

Figure 4.1 The continental slope and potentially extendable EEZ
Source: Author, based on Prescott (2000: 65)

distinguish different types of margins such as "active" and "passive" ones, which do not resemble the ideal type that formed the basis of the definition in the convention text. The attempt to translate a *scientific concept* that was not very well understood at the time into a *legal concept* for the purpose of reaching a consensus on UNCLOS seemed to have led to more contention rather than less. As Monahan argues,

> This model may have created an impression in some framers' minds that there was a definite expression on the surface of the seafloor of the junction between oceanic and continental rocks, and that expression was the foot of the slope. Furthermore, they also formed the impression that the feature was pervasive enough that it could be used as part of the boundary definition.
>
> (Monahan 2004: 95)

As we saw previously, determining the foot of the slope is the crucial procedural step to set the boundaries of the territorial sea (Egede 2004: 158). However, it is nowadays known that,

> Clearly there is no "exact" foot of the slope but a zone in which judgment must be applied to determine the most likely location of this feature that marks the edge of the continent.
>
> (Monahan 2004: 97)

Hence, while delegates at the convention settled the discussion of demarcation, the search for an objective and reliable procedure continues.[21] The shapes of continental margins are formed by plate tectonics, which differ considerably around the globe. This insight thwarts the initial ambition by the convention to effectively limit the unilateral expansion of territorial waters. What is worse, in the end, the Committee on the Limits of the Continental Shelf is required to interpret data provided by states in order to determine a "physical manifestation in the real world of a concept that appears on a diagram" (ibid. 99). In this light, objectivity appears to be an ideal that the makers of the convention sought as a compromise in order to find common ground during their negotiation.

Expertocracy: who gets to participate in the endless re-making of the Law of the Sea?

The trait of "Comtean Positivism", according to which expertocracy matters for UNCLOS, stems from two failed general conferences during the twentieth century, as well as a number of cases brought before the International Court of Justice.[22] These cases helped to establish the notion that the Law of the Sea was potentially a subject to be regulated by an expert body, rather than something over which states struggled as if locked in a Hobbesian state of anarchy. Following UNCLOS, expert bodies perform the Law of the Sea, especially by settling disputes.[23]

The criticism against the objective measurement of the continental shelf, then, takes us full circle and back to the question of how decisions on boundaries are made. During the UNCLOS III conferences, the discussion revolved around the question of whether the Committee on the Limits of the Continental Shelf should make "recommendations" or "decisions" and whether the outcome should be "final and binding" or "final and unalterable", or even "final, binding and conclusive" (Suarez 2008: 77–78). Article 76 nowadays states that the Commission issues "recommendations" that "shall be final and binding". It remains to be seen, however, what happens if a state challenges the evidence submitted by another state and provides its own research results on the position of the foot of the slope or, following the rejection of British claims by the CLCS concerning an extended zone around Ascension Island, what stance a state might take if the recommendation is undesirable. In any case, as the ocean above the seabed outside the exclusive economic zone is not part of the sovereign territory of the coastal state, scientific research cannot be forbidden. Nevertheless, it is costly and hence limits the options of less well-off countries, which have to hire boats for research as well as scientific advisors (Hinz 2011).

A state's findings are forwarded to the CLCS, which is a quasi-secretive body of experts whose task is to decide upon the validity of data. The commission consists of experts from different scientific areas such as geology, geophysics, and hydrography (Suarez 2008: 86), and its geographical composition continues to reflect Cold War constellations, even though equitable geographical representation is standard UN procedure. In the case of the CLCS, this means that most members come from the Group of Asian states, but Eastern and Western Europe combined hold seven positions (Suarez 2008: 86f.).[24] This mixture of expertise and equitable geographical origin may seem appropriate given the complexity of the matter at hand and the need to derive recommendations. In practice, however, it creates problems, as experts in one particular field might not be able to properly interpret data submitted to them by states if that data requires additional expertise. In these cases, members need to rely on the recommendations of their commission colleagues. Even among experts of a certain field, though, there might be differences in training (Hinz 2011). Leaning on George Orwell, in other words, the way the commission is devised means that some members are more expert than others – a constellation that hinders the effective working of the group.[25]

What is more, even though UNCLOS finally started to work in 1994, to date, the relevant institutions still lack expertise concerning the procedures with which submissions are made to the CLCS and what the appropriate way of handling territorial disputes is. Concerning the lack of expertise, the CLCS has produced an instruction manual and also hosted open meetings to lay out requirements of its members (Croker 2004; Hinz 2011).[26] Regarding disputes, it needs to be understood that these may not only concern maritime delimitations but could also involve a challenge to boundaries on land. That is to say, clashes may come in various guises, and the CLCS might not be as willing to deal with them as is the ICJ, for instance (Oude Elfering 2004). In part, this is due to the CLCS having to develop procedural documents from scratch during its first term in office between

1997 and 2002. The technical guidelines were adopted on 13 May 1999, triggering the ten-year period of submission (Croker 2004).

Reasons to tackle disputes head on are multi-faceted and may centre on a lack of expertise in the Commission – bear in mind that it comprises geologists, hydrologists, and so on but not lawyers – as well as a limitation of competence which derives from a lack of explicit mandate in the rules of procedure. In any case, it would be difficult to resolve disputes, as it is not permitted to disclose information to third parties. This is to say that only the state submitting data and the Commission exchange their expertise, while others who might be affected by the outcome have no means to challenge it. As Peter Croker (2004: 218–219) remarked during a special meeting at the UN on 9 December 2002, celebrating the 20th anniversary of opening UNCLOS for signature,

> There is something of a clamor now going on amongst some of the world's scientists who are eager to examine our recommendations to the Russian Federation in detail. However, the Commission's role is clearly stated in the Convention, which is to submit the recommendations in writing to the coastal State which made the submission and to the Secretary-General of the United Nations. There appears to be no mechanism for promulgation of the detailed recommendations from the Commission to any other body.

This reliance on experts, it turns out, may counteract the scope for subsequent challenges to decisions. As in Comte's plans for an ordered and peaceful society, expertise and a lack of possibilities for revision lead to a depoliticisation of life. When it comes to some provisions of the Law of the Sea, politics among people takes place behind closed doors. While this may be conducive to making a decision and is in accordance with Comte's idea of sociocracy, it runs counter to the idea of including all of humanity.

Summary

The intention of sciences was to harmonise, adjust, and regulate the entire system of objective knowledge (Gane 2006: 95) as it applies to natural phenomena as well as society. From the Comtean perspective, it is a consistent move to codify the Law of the Sea and answer Pardo's call for a solution to the tendency towards national appropriation. I pointed out this development with regard to the Truman Proclamation, as well as a number of unilateral moves to extend territorial zones during the 1950s and 1960s. Some observers regarded these moves as the harbinger of an anarchic practice of appropriation – not unlike the situation Comte witnessed during his youth in the decades after 1789. For Comte, the cure to the potential terror of popular sovereignty (Wagner 2001: 33) was to be found in a government of experts. The cure to the random appropriation of the "common heritage of humankind" was to be found in specialised organisations, including the CLCS. During the process of creating UNCLOS, three Comtean principles emerged as the horizons of the participants at the conference fused.

Coming back to the initial puzzle of the chapter, answers to the central question of ownership in contemporary ocean governance are developed behind closed doors and in the cellar room where the CLCS meets. Informality seems to be strongly conducive to the fusion of the horizons of these experts, as it was during the nine years of negotiating UNCLOS. However, from the points of view of those potentially affected by such agreements – that is, the rest of humankind – the lack of transparency of those meetings translates into a missed opportunity to reverse the process.

Should the observer be surprised that experts are granted the task of deciding the limits of the continental shelf? Not at all, if we understand the daily instantiation of the Law of the Sea in terms of the topos that centres on "Comtean Positivism". Objectivity holds that there are no controversial outcomes, because facts supposedly speak for themselves or can be identified by experts. However, a hermeneutic reading of UNCLOS makes us aware of how technocratic solutions inherent to positivism systematically circumvent popular sovereignty in the name of order and stability. Coupled with questions of access, they ultimately undermine the emancipatory intentions that Pardo (and Comte) envisaged.

Conclusion

This chapter has offered an interpretive discussion of the UN Convention on the Law of the Sea. It developed the narrative centring on the topos of "Comtean Positivism" through an interpretive approach that rests on the double hermeneutic, in that it focuses on knowledge creation in day-to-day practices as well as in the work of researchers. The account starts from the premise that hermeneutic encounters are central to global politics. The interpretive focus in this chapter lay on the procedures and settings within which these encounters take place and the kind of prejudgements that shaped the contours of the Law of the Sea Convention. The chapter operationalised what was argued in Chapter 3; that is, that an approach to IR based on the play of performances paves the way for insights without a priori assumptions about preferences and that it is conducive to explaining processes. In this way, this chapter furthers existing constructivist research in IR by illustrating how a focus on developments over time can be accomplished.

However, operationalising a double hermeneutic approach was only one of two aims. As the chapter engages in problem-oriented theory-building, it also furthers a better understanding of ocean governance. By abductively reconstructing a topos from publicly available sources, the topos of "Comtean Positivism" explains the Law of the Sea in terms of a particular trajectory. This codification of the Law of the Sea in UNCLOS, and its current development, are marked by a commitment to expertocracy, humanity, and objectivity. As the topos explains what has happened to the Law of the Sea and why, its reconstruction marks a first step towards engaging normative questions of global politics. While some scholars merely ask whether there is a "'Democratic Deficit' in World Politics" (Moravcsik 2004), the reconstructive analysis presented in this chapter is able to characterise more specifically what is happening in contemporary ocean governance. At its core, in the case of UNCLOS, it involves questions of knowledge creation and accessing situations in which people not only "make sense", for instance, of the data submitted to an organisation like the CLCS or of certain concepts such as the continental shelf, but also "make worlds". As far as the ongoing making of sense and worlds is concerned (compare Onuf 1989), on the basis of the analysis conducted in this chapter, it is possible to conclude that the Law of the Sea is characterised by an increasing reliance on methods of natural sciences as well as unquestionable expertise, which makes it difficult, if not impossible, to preserve the "common heritage of humankind" as an accessible space. The reliance on expertocracy and the quest for objectivity depoliticises ocean governance, on the one hand, but may also come at the expense of excluding humanity at large, on the other.

Recognising this trajectory, which can be offered as a hypothetical conclusion to the discussion of UNCLOS presented in this chapter, marks a first step in engaging with the questions of global governance that are concerned with legitimate governance and institution-building in settings beyond the state (Zürn 2000; Steffek 2008; Jönsson and Tallberg 2010; Albert 2016; Wiener 2018; Zürn 2018). Further research could venture towards discovering topoi in other regimes so as to derive a typology of regimes which lends itself to systematic comparison. Another possibility would entail using the topos of "Comtean Positivism" as a hypothesis for enquiries into other regimes that address the possessions of humankind, such as Space Law. However, since that was not the concern of this chapter, nor of this book, I postpone this undertaking for another day.

Notes

1 Platzöder (1982) and later publications are the prime sources of documents from which it is possible to reconstruct the negotiations.
2 While acknowledging that the Law of the Sea comprises more than UNCLOS, most of the discussion concerns aspects closely related to how UNCLOS emerged and contributed to the Law of the Sea. By September 2013, UNCLOS had been signed by 168 states; compare: www.un.org/depts/los/reference_files/chronological_lists_of_ratifi cations.htm [accessed 1 June 2019].
3 The flag was planted on 2 August 2007; see http://news.bbc.co.uk/2/hi/europe/6927395. stm [accessed 3 June 2019]. Recent activities follow a century-old discussion between proponents of the concept of *mare liberum* (published by Hugo Grotius in 1609) and the advocates of the principle of *mare clausum* (advocated by John Selden in 1635), which contain antagonistic ideas about sovereign rights, possession, and general use of coastal waters and the high seas. It is currently part of the argument advanced in the most recent case of the International Tribunal for the Law of the Sea. Compare the *Arctic Sunrise* case, for which documentation is available online: www.itlos.org/index. php?id=264 [accessed 3 June 2019].
4 See also: www.reuters.com/article/2012/07/27/us-denmark-greenland-northpole-idUSBRE86Q10O20120727 [accessed 4 June 2019].
5 See www.bbc.co.uk/news/world-asia-pacific-11341139 [accessed 1 June 2019].
6 The third conference on the Law of the Sea lasted from 1973–1982. Previous attempts to codify the Law of the Sea had taken place in The Hague in 1930. Two previous conferences in 1958 and 1960 only settled aspects of the law.
7 The study is therefore not a discussion of the current perspective of international law, nor of the Law of the Sea in its entirety. Rather, I focus on its trajectory during the

latter part of the twentieth century and the performances contributing to codifying the Law of the Sea in the third conference. I also take into account current instantiations whenever they help illustrate my argument.

8   For instance, there seems to be disagreement in the scholarly community concerning the exact timing of the third session, which took place in Geneva in 1975. While Suarez (2008: 48) writes that the session took place between 17 March and 9 May 1975, Jagota (1985) and Stevenson and Oxman (1975) place it between 26 March and 10 May. Among the same group of authors, there is further disagreement concerning the exact dates of a meeting period including session five, which took place in New York. Jagota (1985) dates the session from 2 August to 17 September 1976, while Oxman (1977) has it finishing a week earlier. These may be minor remarks, but they remind us to be careful when using sources.

9   Such speech acts may be the teachings of international lawyers; compare Article 38(1d) of the Statute of the ICJ, which specifies that "the teachings of the most qualified publicists of the various nations" are among the sources of international law. Other sources listed are international conventions, international custom, and principles of law available online: www.icj-cij.org/documents/?p1=4&p2=2&p3=0#CHAPTER_ II [accessed 4 June 2019].

10 UN Doc. A/CONF.62/30/Rev.2, at 8–10, 17 (1976), reprinted in Buzan (1981: 347).

11 Gerhard Wagner (2001: 97–99) and also Yvonne Bernart (2003: 40) argue that recent social theories, particularly systems theory and world society approaches by Parsons and Luhmann, do not sufficiently acknowledge their Comtean legacy. What is more, they contain a teleological understanding of progress. While they might have replaced Herbert Spencer's idea of social Darwinism and progress with a modest version of evolution, ultimately the idea of (functional) progress which *inevitably* applies to and spans all humankind is still present. Gane (2006: 12) argues that this even applies to postmodern approaches who "find their ideas haunted by progressive frameworks (that is, they are post-)".

12 For instance, in 1849, Comte devised a positivist calendar that drew on concepts of the revolutionary calendar as far as the division of months and weeks was concerned. Starting in 1789, a year would contain 13 months of 28 days. However, Comte borrows also from Catholic principles by assigning each day to a (secular) saint (Wagner 2001: 66–70).

13 The idea of sociocracy stands in contrast to democracy. While the latter refers to the government of the masses, Comte's concept envisages the government of people who have an affectionate relation with each other (Wagner 2001: 86). In this regard, his distinction mirrors other social theorists who are critical of social developments in the nineteenth century, who called for a more organic bond between people. Ferdinand Tönnies's distinction between *Gemeinschaft* and *Gesellschaft* may serve as an example.

14 Comte assigns women a predominantly conservative role. They are to fulfil a caring function and hence balance the otherwise sober and male secular order (Gane 2006: 4). The proletariat is deemed particularly suitable to be governed because it did not obtain any education in metaphysics – it is a tabula rasa in this regard (Gane 2006: 5; Lepenies 2010: 161).

15 Interview with Renate Platzöder, 18 September 2011. Further, the concept of "heritage" is mentioned in similar form in the 1954 "Hague Convention for the Protection of Cultural Property in the Event of Armed Conflict", cf. http://portal.unesco.org/en/ev.php-URL_ID=13637&URL_DO=DO_TOPIC&URL_SECTION=201.html [accessed 4 June 2019].

16 For an early sceptical voice against Pardo's optimism, see Ernst Haas's analysis (1975).

17 Sanger (1986: 25) quotes US ambassador Leigh Ratiner, accordingly: "[Throughout the entire negotiation process] Canada was always a friend of developing countries".

18 For extensive commentary see Suarez (2008) and Harrison (2011). The Truman Proclamation can be found online: www.trumanlibrary.org. The official citation is 10 Fed. Reg. 12305 (1945) (Executive Order 9633 of 28 September 1945).

19 This claim was made in the so-called Santiago Declaration of 1952 by Chile, Ecuador, and Peru; see Heidar (2004: 21).
20 For the adopted convention text on the Continental Shelf (Article 76), see Renate Platzöder's publication of the convention's documents (1982, Vol. III: 46–47).
21 In this regard, consider the recent rejection by the Commission on the Limits of the Continental Shelf of British claims to an exclusive economic zone beyond 200 nm around Ascension Island (Serdy 2013).
22 The conventions took place in 1958 and 1960, respectively. Court cases established principles of friendly passage, as in the *Corfu Channel* case, and dispute settlement in cases of boundary disputes (*North Sea Continental Shelf*), as well as technical procedures for demarcating territorial waters (*Fisheries Case*).
23 But consider the recent abstention from the *Arctic Sunrise* case by the Russian Federation.
24 The delegation comprises the following: four members from the Group of African States, six from the Group of Asian States, three from Eastern Europe, four from Latin American and Caribbean states, and four from Western European and other states.
25 Another problematic issue arises from the discussion over expenses and emoluments (Suarez 2008: 88f.). As states that nominate members of the commission have to take over their emoluments, there is an occasional lack of enthusiasm to provide financial support.
26 The complicated nature of preparing a proper submission and the lack of expertise around the globe mean that former members of CLCS are much sought after to work as advisors.

References

Albert, M. (2016). *A Theory of World Politics*. Cambridge, Cambridge University Press.
Baker, B. (2011). Uncommon Heritage: Elisabeth Mann Borgese, Pacem in Maribus, the International Ocean Institute and Preparations for UNCLOS III. *Ocean Yearbook* **26**(1): 11–34.
Barkin, J. S. and E. R. DeSombre (2013). *Saving Global Fisheries: Reducing Fishing Capacity to Promote Sustainability*. Cambridge, MA, The MIT Press.
Berkman, P. A., L. Kullerud, A. Pope, A. N. Vylegzhanin and O. R. Young (2017). The Arctic Science Agreement Propels Science Diplomacy. *Science* **358**(6363): 596–598.
Bernart, Y. (2003). *Der Beitrag des erfahrungswissenschaftlichen Positivismus in der Tradition Auguste Comtes zur Genese der Soziologie: Rekonstruktion exemplarischer Entwicklungsrichtlinen*. Göttingen, Cuvillier.
Buzan, B. (1981). Negotiating by Consensus: Developments in Technique at the United Nations Conference on the Law of the Sea. *American Journal of International Law* **75**(4): 324–348.
Byers, M. (2009). *Who Owns the Arctic?* Vancouver, Douglas & McIntyre.
Croker, P. F. (2004). The Commission on the Limits of the Continental Shelf: Progress to Date and Future Challenges. *Legal and Scientific Aspects of Continental Shelf Limits*. M. H. Nordquist, J. Norton Moore and T. H. Heidar. Leiden and Boston, Martinus Nijhoff Publishers: 215–221.
Dodds, K. (2010). Flag Planting and Finger Pointing: The Law of the Sea, the Arctic and the Political Geographies of the Outer Continental Shelf. *Political Geography* **29**(2): 63–73.
Egede, E. (2004). The Outer Limits of the Continental Shelf: African States and the 1982 Law of the Sea Convention. *Ocean Development & International Law* **35**(2): 157–178.
Eustis, R. D. (1977). Note: Procedures and Techniques of Multinational Negotiation: The LOS III Model. *Virginia Journal of International Law* **17**: 217–256.

Friedmann, W. (1973). Selden *Redivivus* – Towards a Partition of the Seas? *American Journal of International Law* **65**(4): 757–770.
Gane, M. (2006). *Auguste Comte*. London, Routledge.
Haas, E. B. (1975). Is There a Hole in the Whole? Knowledge, Technology, Interdependence, and the Construction of International Regimes. *International Organization* **29**(3): 827–876.
Haas, E. B. (1980). Why Collaborate? Issue-Linkage and International Regimes. *World Politics* **32**(3): 357–405.
Harrison, J. (2011). *Making the Law of the Sea: A Study in the Development of International Law*. Cambridge, Cambridge University Press.
Heidar, T. H. (2004). Legal Aspects of the Continental Shelf Limits. *Legal and Scientific Aspects of the Continental Shelf Limits*. M. H. Nordquist, J. Norton Moore and T. H. Heidar. Leiden and Boston, Martinus Nejhoff Publishers: 19–40.
Higgins, R. (1995). *Problems and Process – International Law and How We Use It*. Oxford, Oxford University Press.
Hinz, K. (2011). Wem gehört die zentrale Arktis? Geologie, Bathymetrie und das Seerecht. *Osteuropa* **61**(2–3): 87–92.
Jagota, S. P. (1985). *Maritime Boundary*. Dordrecht, Martinus Nijhoff.
Jönsson, C. and J. Tallberg, Eds. (2010). *Transnational Actors in Global Governance: Patterns, Explanations, and Implications*. Basingstoke, Palgrave Macmillan.
Keil, K. (2014). The Arctic: A New Region of Conflict? The Case of Oil and Gas. *Cooperation and Conflict* **49**(2): 162–190.
Keohane, R. O. (1984). *After Hegemony. Cooperation and Discord in the World Political Economy*. Princeton, NJ, Princeton University Press.
Klabbers, J. (2006). The Meaning of Rules. *International Relations* **20**(3): 295–301.
Koh, T. (1983). A Constitution for the Oceans. *The Law of the Sea: United Nations Convention on the Law of the Sea*. New York, St. Martin's Press.
Larson, D. L., M. W. Roth and T. I. Selig (1995). An Analysis of the Ratification of the UN Convention on the Law of the Sea. *Ocean Development & International Law* **26**(3): 287–303.
Lasswell, H. D. (1990). *Politics: Who Gets What, When and How*. Gloucester, Peter Smith Publisher Inc.
Lepenies, W. (2010). *Auguste Comte: die Macht der Zeichen*. München, Hanser.
Manley, R. H. (1979). Developing Nation Imperatives for a New Law of the Sea: UNCLOS I and III as Stages in the International Policy Process. *Ocean Development & International Law* **7**(1–2): 9–18.
Monahan, D. (2004). Determining the Foot of the Continental Slope as the Point of Maximum Change in the Gradient at Its Base. *Legal and Scientific Aspects of the Continental Shelf Limits*. M. H. Nordquist, J. Norton Moore and T. H. Heidar. Leiden and Boston, Martinus Nijhoff Publishers: 91–120.
Moravcsik, A. (2004). Is There a 'Democratic Deficit' in World Politics? A Framework for Analysis. *Government and Opposition* **39**(2): 336–363.
Nordquist, M. H., J. Norton Moore, A. Chircop and R. Long, Eds. (2013). *The Regulation of Continental Shelf Development – Rethinking International Standards*. Leiden, Martinus Nijhoff.
Onuf, N. (1989). *World of Our Making: Rules and Rule in Social Theory and International Relations*. Columbia, University of South Carolina Press.
Oude Elfering, A. G. (2004). Submissions of Coastal States to the CLCS in Cases of Unresolved Land or Maritime Disputes. *Legal and Scientific Aspects of Continental Shelf Limits*. M. H. Nordquist, J. Norton Moore and T. H. Heidar. Leiden and Boston, Martinus Nijhoff Publishers: 263–285.

Oxman, B. H. (1977). The Third United Nations Conference on the Law of the Sea: The 1976 New York Sessions. *American Journal of International Law* **71**(2): 247–269.

Oxman, B. H. (1978). The Third United Nations Conference on the Law of the Sea: The 1977 New York Session. *American Journal of International Law* **72**(1): 57–83.

Oxman, B. H. (1979). The Third United Nations Conference on the Law of the Sea: The Seventh Session (1978). *American Journal of International Law* **73**(1): 1–41.

Oxman, B. H. (1980). The Third United Nations Conference on the Law of the Sea: The Eighth Session (1979). *American Journal of International Law* **74**(1): 1–47.

Oxman, B. H. (1981). The Third United Nations Conference on the Law of the Sea: The Ninth Session (1980). *American Journal of International Law* **75**(2): 211–256.

Oxman, B. H. (1982). Introduction: On Evaluating the Draft Convention on the Law of the Sea. *San Diego Law Review* **19**(3): 453–460.

Oxman, B. H. (1995). International Maritime Boundaries: Political, Strategic and Historical Considerations. *University of Miam Inter-American Law Review* **26**: 243–295.

Oxman, B. H. (1996). The Rule of Law and the United Nations Convention on the Law of the Sea. *European Journal of International Law* **7**(3): 353–371.

Pardo, A. (1967). *Speech at the UN General Assembly, 1515th Meeting (1 November 1967)*. New York available online: www.un.org/Depts/los/convention_agreements/texts/pardo_ga1967.pdf.

Platzöder, R., Ed. (1982, Vol. III). *Third United Nations Conference on the Law of the Sea: Documents*. Dobbs Ferry, Oceana.

Prescott, V. (2000). Resources of the Continental Margin and International Law. *Continental Shelf Limits: The Scientific and Legal Interface*. P. J. Cook and C. M. Carleton. Oxford, Oxford University Press: 64–83.

Rolshausen, C. (2001). Auguste Comte. *Schlüsselwerke der Soziologie*. G. W. Oesterdiekhoff and S. Papke. Wiesbaden, Westdeutscher Verlag: 89–91.

Rothwell, D. R. and T. Stephens (2010). *The International Law of the Sea*. Oxford and Portland, Hart Publishing.

Sanger, C. (1986). *Ordering the Oceans: The Making of the Law of the Sea*. London, Zed Books.

Serdy, A. (2013). Interpretation of UNCLOS Article 76 and the Negative Recommendation of the Commission on the Limits of the Continental Shelf on Ascension Island: Is the United Kingdom Stuck with It? *Cambridge Journal of International and Comparative Law* **2**(3): 591–611.

Steffek, J. (2008). *Civil Society Participation in European and Global Governance: A Cure for the Democratic Deficit?* Basingstoke, Palgrave Macmillan.

Steinberg, P. E. (2001). *The Social Construction of the Ocean*. Cambridge, Cambridge University Press.

Stevenson, J. R. and B. H. Oxman (1974). The Preparations for the Law of the Sea Conference. *American Journal of International Law* **68**(1): 1–32.

Stevenson, J. R. and B. H. Oxman (1975). The Third United Nations Conference on the Law of the Sea: The 1975 Geneva Session. *American Journal of International Law* **69**(4): 763–797.

Suarez, S. V. (2008). *The Outer Limits of the Continental Shelf: Legal Aspects of Their Establishment*. Berlin and New York, Springer.

Tiller, R. and E. Nyman (2018). Ocean Plastics and the BBNJ Treaty – Is Plastic Frightening Enough to Insert Itself into the BBNJ Treaty, or Do We Need to Wait for a Treaty of Its Own? *Journal of Environmental Studies and Sciences* **8**(4): 411–415.

Wagner, G. (2001). *Auguste Comte – zur Einführung*. Hamburg, Junius.

Waltz, K. N. (1979). *Theory of International Politics*. New York, McGraw-Hill.

Webster, D. G. (2015). *Beyond the Tragedy: Evolution and Sustainability in Global Fisheries Governance*. Cambridge, MA, The MIT Press.

Wiener, A. (2018). *Constitution and Contestation of Norms in Global International Relations*. Cambridge, Cambridge University Press.

Wolf, K. D. (1981). *Die Dritte Seerechtskonferenz der Vereinten Nationen: Beiträge zur Reform der internationalen Ordnung und Entwicklungstendenzen im Nord-Süd-Verhältnis*. Baden-Baden, Nomos.

Wolf, K. D. (1991). *Internationale Regime zur Verteilung globaler Ressourcen: Eine vergleichende Analyse der Grundlage Ihrer Entstehung am Beispiel der Regelung des Zugangs zur wirtschaftlichen Nutzung des Meeresbodens, des geostationären Orbits, der Antarktis und Wissenschaften und Technologies*. Baden-Baden, Nomos.

Wood-Donnelly, C. (2019). *Performing Arctic Sovereignty: Policy and Visual Narratives*. London and New York, Routledge.

Zürn, M. (2000). Democratic Governance Beyond the Nation-State: The EU and Other International Institutions. *European Journal of International Relations* 6(2): 183–221.

Zürn, M. (2018). *A Theory of Global Governance – Authority, Legitimacy & Contestation*. Oxford, Oxford University Press.

5 Humanity and German intervention in Kosovo 1999

The case: intervention and the concern for humanity

This chapter has two aims. First, it illustrates the hermeneutic methodology advanced in previous chapters. The empirical starting point differs from the UNCLOS study in that now personal and collective horizons take centre stage, though the operationalisation of the research will follow the same criteria as explained in Chapter 3. Second, the chapter makes an argument concerning the normative composition of contemporary global politics by investigating the politics among people that shaped German politics in the 1990s, which in itself is a small piece of the puzzle of the changing understanding of sovereignty in a global context.[1] State-focused approaches have addressed the issue of a changing understanding of sovereignty, particularly through studies of humanitarian intervention and human rights norms. In contrast to these studies, which often take the UN framework as the source of origin for the global spread of these norms, the particular case presented in this chapter explains that a commitment to liberty, equality, tolerance, and dignity – embedded in "politics among people" and developed through hermeneutic encounters – can account for a small but important part of their development. Working out the central topos of German foreign policy in the late 1990s, an engagement with the politics of hermeneutic encounters makes the case's long-term impact on international relations comprehensible because it focuses on human agency and the continuous spinning of a web of meaning. As I will explain subsequently, a play of performances centring on the topos of "Humanity" explains the transformation of lessons from history, thereby enabling alternative policies towards questions of war, peace, and intervention.

The question of (non-)intervention, state sovereignty, and responsibility towards others continues to be at the heart of IR (Bartelson 1995; Aalberts 2004; Glanville 2014) and is embedded in a play of performances (Ringmar 2018; Wood-Donnelly 2019). This chapter addresses a part of the trajectory of humanitarian intervention, with a particular focus on German involvement during the early stages of what would later become known as the "responsibility to protect" (RtoP).[2] The climax of the particular play addressed in this chapter occurred in spring 1999, when NATO began bombing the first targets in Yugoslavia on 24 March 1999 during its so-called Operation Allied Force.[3] Six months after coming into office, the newly formed government of Social Democrats and the Green Party committed German troops to participate in the mission – although no obvious national interests were at stake, although the participation contradicted German policies of the past, and although it was contrary to the very ideals for which the parties, especially the Green Party, had long since fought.

Based on this puzzle, this chapter enquires in analogous fashion to the study conducted in the previous chapter. It asks what performances enabled the intervention and what conclusions can be drawn regarding the normative composition of contemporary global politics. By focusing on hermeneutic encounters and following the methodology outlined in Chapter 3, it is possible to conclude that, at least during the early days of RtoP, a concern for humanity can explain the German participation in the mission and also account for the development of sovereignty and states' responsibility towards other states' citizens.

While the chapter focuses on the puzzling role of Germany, the broader setting of the military engagement is a particularly interesting case for IR because it is taken to have established the precursor of the international legal norm of RtoP, through which so-called humanitarian interventions can be legitimised in the context of international law (Lepard 2002; Wheeler 2002, 2006).[4] RtoP was referred to in UN Security Council Resolution 1973 in connection with Chapter VII of the UN Charter on 17 March 2011, after which US-led forces first established a no-fly zone in Libya and subsequently contributed to the overthrow of the Libyan government.[5] It is thus safe to say that RtoP has become a firm point of reference in international politics and occupies a key role in contemporary global normative order, even though its status in legal terms is subject to debate (Welsh and Banda 2010).

With a view to explaining the recent trajectory of this order, I focus on the German involvement in NATO's Operation Allied Force. The operation is puzzling for IR scholarship: because of the problems that realist explanations face, given that no immediate gains in terms of security or well-being could be anticipated or derived from the action, scholars have largely reverted to addressing aspects of the "strategic" or "foreign policy culture" (Lantis 2002; Longhurst 2004; Dalgaard-Nielsen 2005; Pradetto 2006; Stahl 2008). This scholarship seeks to address a change in the German outlook on military engagement and intervention, which ran counter to the established identitarian dimension of German foreign policy, characterised by restraint since WWII (Rathbun 2006; Leithner 2009; Brunstetter and Brunstetter 2011). What is more, it stood in stark contrast to the prevailing position of the government at the time. Particularly, the Green Party (the Greens) had strong roots in anti-military and anti-nuclear social movements whose pacifist position stemmed from the conviction that a post-WWII Germany must never engage in war again.[6] The government's (and parliament's) decision to participate in NATO's mission is thus even more puzzling if we consider that it had no mandate from the UN Security Council and did not qualify as a *casus foederis* under Article 5 of the North Atlantic Treaty.[7] In addition to the legal arguments, it is worth reminding ourselves that the Greens had campaigned for Germany to leave NATO until the mid-1990s (Volmer 1998: 102).[8]

However, even though the focus is on matters of identity and culture, the operationalisation of this issue for research lacks a focus on the hermeneutic encounters that explain its shift. Addressed in terms of "politics among people", drawing conclusions from voting behaviour in parliament or opinion polls is insufficient. Some constructivists predominantly look for cross-national convergence of policies based on the UN framework enabling humanitarian intervention by *states* (Finnemore 1996b; Risse and Sikkink 1999; for a critique, see Rathbun 2004: 6). Indeed, a considerable part of the discussion of German foreign policy in the late 1990s adopts a state-level approach (Baumann and Hellmann 2001) or ascribes changes in policy to the impact of individuals (Hyde-Price 2001). While they provide empirical context, these approaches tend to gloss over how understandings of particular situations are social interpretations and webs of meaning that are collectively spun, as explained in Chapter 2. What is required is an approach to identity that does not merely consider it an independent variable for explaining state behaviour (Nabers 2018). Considering the hermeneutic embeddedness of foreign policy making, the perspective of IR as politics among people allows me to reconstruct a specific case in which the main protagonists underwent a literally painstaking process to arrive at what they deemed a moral and decent decision.

The importance of the role of people and their hermeneutic encounters is sometimes hinted at in the literature but rarely followed up with empirical assessment (Pradetto 2006: 24). While the dictum "never again Auschwitz" was certainly important in the transformation of Green foreign policy (e.g. Brunstetter and Brunstetter 2011), the case study to follow shows that it was not the accepted position in the party at the beginning of the war in Yugoslavia, and it was certainly not clear what kind of policy should follow from adopting it. By reconstructing the topos of "Humanity" from publicly available sources, the chapter explains how nonviolence became regarded as an end, rather than a means, of politics – particularly of German foreign policy.

More specifically, following the methodology and method discussed in Chapter 3, I argue that the puzzle of German participation can be solved if we understand how key members of the Green Party came to reconcile their "horizon". While the horizon used to be characterised by the dictum "never again war", during the second half of the 1990s, it changed into a concern for ending suffering, drawing particularly on the collective memory of Nazi atrocities in the 1930s and 1940s (Baumann and Hellmann 2001; Kundnani 2009; Leithner 2009; Brunstetter and Brunstetter 2011). I argue that the topos of "Humanity", as discussed in more detail subsequently, helps us understand how and why it was possible to engage in a military mission that had no mandate by the United Nations. This concern for humanity was still connected to the past in that it regarded German atrocities of the 1940s as an ethical mandate not to let anything similar happen again. Critically, however, the new position now entailed that passivity or a rigorous rejection of military means was no longer the only option. As the examples will reveal, for IR, the implication is that such a change in perspective is difficult to achieve and sometimes literally painful.

The remainder of the chapter is organised as follows. First, I outline the methodology of the case study. This section is considerably shorter than the corresponding section in the previous chapter, because I proceeded in the same way and therefore the approach does not require repeating. In the following section, I introduce the core features of the topos of "Humanity", the meta-narrative that explains the play of performances in the context of this case study. As in the previous chapter, the topos was abductively reconstructed from the analysis of sources and not deductively applied to my data. Yet, in analogous fashion to the previous chapter, I begin with the result to allow the readers to better trace the analysis.

Next, I outline the context of the case. This section centres on the trajectory of the party and its members. I sketch the Greens' origins in the social movements of the 1960s and later decades and also outline the contours of the party in the 1990s. I show that elements of "Humanity" were present in the party and among its members from the beginning. This presence accounts for a constitutively causal trajectory towards German participation in NATO's mission, since it marks the horizon on the basis of which performances were possible.

With regard to the actual case study, the following section shows how activists and their phronetic knowledge have become part of the performances of the German state. The topos of "Humanity" explains how it was possible for them to gradually draw *new* lessons from the German past. In regard to NATO intervention in Kosovo, the resulting performances shaped Germany's foreign policy. While I *do not* entertain the argument that the Greens (or Germany, for that matter) were directly responsible for the creation of RtoP, I *do* argue that it was an important, if only small, contribution to altering the contours of sovereignty and the norms of non-intervention. After all, the reference points to genocide have become established topoi in connection with the reconsideration of sovereignty in the international arena and the associated responsibilities of the United Nations (Pradetto 2014; Niemann 2019).

With regard to approaching international relations as politics among people, I conclude that a change in perspective and broadening of horizons, such as ones that mark the trajectory of Green foreign policy since the mid-1990s, is not a project that people undertake lightly. People, and thus states, do not simply discover new preferences which they follow consequentially. Formulating policy in accordance with the principles of "Humanity" was not a self-fulfilling trajectory. With regard to IR theory, I conclude that a perspective of "politics among people" is indeed a fruitful and a possible alternative approach, for two reasons. First, it can address a problem that state-centric approaches cannot solve, and second, it is able to explain the *process* of the hard struggle that people underwent to make what they deemed an ethical decision.

Outline of the case study: data and the process of analysis

The case study proceeds by the same method as applied in the previous chapter and adheres to the same criteria of validity. Regarding the data used for the study, I reconstruct the topos of "Humanity" from relying on publicly available sources such as speeches in the Bundestag, but also on interview statements and narrative accounts from key members of the Greens. Following the method discussed in Chapter 4, I abductively derived themes and eventually the topos of "Humanity", whose explanatory power I illustrate subsequently.

By analogy to the previous case, the topos was not a conclusion that was immediately obvious because other potential topoi were conceivable until the end of the analysis. One candidate was "Christianity" due to its emphasis on compassion. However, this quality alone was difficult to justify as sufficient for a topos, particularly given that the "love thy neighbour" dictum originates from the Book of Leviticus in the Old Testament and hence could be seen as belonging to Jewish tradition. What is more, not enough empirical evidence was available to sustain the argument that intervention was based on religious motives. Another possible topos was that of "Civilisation". This has repeatedly been identified as a central component in interventions at different points in time, justifying action by recourse to an allegedly superior state of development and the offering of assistance to the underdeveloped, such as during the discovery of the Americas (Jahn 2000) or the war in Vietnam (Milliken and Sylvan 1996). Regarding the Balkan War[9] of the 1990s, Lene Hansen has reconstructed the civilisational relation between European countries and the Balkans in the nineteenth and early twentieth centuries and points out that this was, in part, the relevant topos during the 1990s (Hansen 2006: Chapters 6 and 7).[10] Nevertheless, while this topos may have mattered in the context of the debate in the United States and the United Kingdom, the argument could not be sustained with regard to the German engagement. "Humanity", as explained subsequently, provides a more encompassing explanation for the development of German foreign policy under the Green Party's leadership.

A methodological difference between this and the previous chapter concerns the horizon from which the topos is reconstructed. Whereas in the case of UNCLOS, previous legislation and failed conferences marked the contextual horizon and the available stock of knowledge from which conference delegates could draw, the situation is different in the case of the Greens. Here, it is the Gadamerian "effective history" embodied by members of the party, acquired and shaped through decades of activism, which matters most. It is therefore important to sketch the contours of the party's trajectory, as I do subsequently in the section titled "Founding the Greens". Familiarity with this development allows me to argue that effective history is not external to the protagonists but touches upon the very essence of their identity. This explains why the overall play of performance developing a position on the war in the Balkans was marked by an intense debate and sometimes even by physical confrontation among party members.

To briefly illustrate the broader conceptual argument, the focus is limited to the role of social movements of the 1960s and the early days of the Green Party before it formed part of the German government coalition at the time of NATO intervention in Kosovo in 1999. The aim is not to provide a new account of what happened where, when, and how in the Balkans, as this has been expertly done by others (Lepard 2002; Wheeler 2002; Hansen 2006; Wheeler 2006; Havercroft 2012). Neither do I engage in a debate with current discussions on "democratic peace theory" (Brunstetter and Brunstetter 2011). While recent turns in that debate have shifted the focus from "democratic peace" to "democratic war" in light of increased engagement by democracies in war since 1990 (Geis 2006: 26), such debate would require a cross-national comparative assessment which I do not offer or aim for at this point.

Rather, the emphasis will be on the interpretation of a responsibility towards humanity that stemmed from an active engagement with the past. In this regard, the case study further illustrates an aspect of German policy making that other authors have highlighted as well, that is, that traumatic memories of WWII continue to matter (Berger 1997; Longhurst 2004; Langenbacher 2005; Zehfuss 2007; Kundnani 2009; Brunstetter and Brunstetter 2011; Wüstenberg 2017). These memories have become transgenerational in Assmann's sense, but the intention here is to go beyond the immediate realm of German politics and illustrate how people's fusion of horizons as an activity of "making sense" can have an impact on international relations. It illustrates that "politics among people" matters for the making of global politics.

The topos of "Humanity"

"Humanity" is the topos that explains the surprising involvement of Germany in NATO's Operation Allied Force and the subsequent development of RtoP. Like the topos of "Comtean Positivism" in the previous chapter, "Humanity" also requires a brief explanation. I begin with the emergence of notions of humanity in Early Modern Europe before I review its role in recent discussions in international law as well as IR. The discussion in international law offers nuanced positions from which conceptual definitions can be drawn, whereas scholars of IR have either discussed the concept of "human rights" (and not the concept of "humanity") or present a teleological narrative which is not compatible with the approach presented in this book.

In the context of this book, humanity was previously mentioned as part of Comte's social theory through which it becomes possible to make sense of current ocean governance. However, there is more than one way to consider humanity, and not in all accounts has it been used in terms of a broader, normative social theory. Humanity is rather a theme that has been reflected upon prominently in (European) philosophy at least since the end of the Middle Ages, when newly discovered lands and peoples, as well as new perspectives and conceptualisations of space, redefined the demarcation of polities and the understanding of how humans relate to each other and to their surroundings (Ruggie 1993; Reinhard 1999; Jahn 2000; Lebow 2009).

Artists of the Renaissance, particularly from the fifteenth century such as Leonardo da Vinci and Michelangelo, but also political theorists like Niccolo Machiavelli, increasingly related back to ancient Greek philosophy and art as well as Latin thinkers, notably Cicero. Renaissance humanism was a diverse intellectual development that put the human being at the centre of attention and sought a variety of expressions of what it meant to be human (Holenstein 2004: 114).[11] The points of distinction were usually non-civilised creatures, including animals but also "barbarians" (Teitel 2011: 24). In the sixteenth and seventeenth centuries, humanity increasingly became the subject of discussion in law, Hugo Grotius's *On the Law of War and Peace* being one example in which Grotius appeals to universal principles informing human interaction based on equality and tolerance of the uniting human qualities (Teitel 2011: 23).[12] The discussion of humanity entailed an underlying wish to end religious wars and establish a golden age marked by a society that allowed for a maximum of personal development through compassion, mercy, and reason (Ward 2003: 3–5). The ideal was also discussed during the Enlightenment, notably in Immanuel Kant's treatment of dignity and tolerance as guidelines of human conduct, and remains a recurring point of discussion among contemporary philosophers such as Hannah Arendt and Martha Nussbaum (Burke 2011: 102).[13] In short, "Humanity" as a topos concerns questions about the status of the human being, centring on liberty, equality, tolerance, and dignity (Ward 2003: 123). As summarised in the subsequent table (Table 5.1), Ruti Teitel even goes so far as to say that "[t]he humanity norm refers to both the manner and means of human conduct, and to its ends; the human is a subject and a standard of treatment" (Teitel 2011: 20).

This dual quality as both a subject and a standard of treatment has been, and remains, a prominent topic of debate in the realm of international law. By comparison, the debate in international relations is less critical and less foundational. In contemporary international law, humanity has increasingly become a point of reference, particularly after the founding of the Red Cross and the first of the Geneva Conventions in 1864. The 1899 Hague Convention explicitly aimed to set limits to warfare, making references to principles or laws of humanity in what is known as the Martens Clause (Rensmann 2008: 112; Teitel 2011: 26).[14] The clause closes legal loopholes by stating that in the absence of more encompassing laws, "populations and belligerents remain under the protection and empire of the principles of international law, as they result from the usages established between civilised nations, from the laws of humanity, and the requirements of the public conscience" (Meron 2000: 79).[15]

The general references to laws of humanity and also to public conscience allowed jurists to draw on positive (written) law and customary law when making arguments about human rights and further fill the concept of "humanity" with meaning. Regarding crimes against humanity, crimes against individual persons are judged to have occurred according to group characteristics that are out of the person's control. Hence there is a "strong forward assault on that person's humanity. It is as if the individuality of that person were being ignored, and the

Table 5.1 The dual character of "Humanity"

"Humanity"	1) Subject 2) Standard of treatment	Traits: liberty, equality, tolerance, dignity

Source: Author, based on Ward (2003) and Teitel (2011)

person were being treated as a mere representative of a group that the person has not chosen to join" (May 2005: 85). Recent developments since 1999 have arguably moved international law further towards an "individual-centred, humanised system" (Cassese 2000: 216; Chandler 2001; Peters 2009: 514; Gholiagha 2015) in which the responsibility to protect has "definitely ousted the principle of sovereignty from its position as a *Letztbegründung* (first principle) of international law [. . . to the extent that humanity is] the *telos* of the international legal system. Humanity is the A and Ω of sovereignty" (Peters 2009: 514, emphasis in original).[16]

From these developments, one may get the impression that humanity is a well-established and generally recognised part of international law and, by extension, international politics. Indeed, scholars of IR have discussed the power of human rights and its persistence (Risse, Ropp et al. 1999, 2013). However, there is a bias in the discussion in that authors seem to take the telos of human rights as given and mostly enquire into cross-national policy convergence. Authors discuss the role of human rights as a positive development of liberal institutions through the work of norm entrepreneurs, such as humanitarian NGOs (Finnemore and Sikkink 1998), but particularly embrace a perspective that begins with the adoption of the Universal Declaration of Human Rights by the UN General Assembly (Risse and Sikkink 1999: 1). In terms of methodology, this approach is interested in explaining state behaviour, taking the norm of human rights as its independent variable. Thus, a methodological problem is the separation context and performance (or, in their wording, state action) in order to explain the latter by the former (Finnemore 1996b). Authors thereby conflate the *telos* of humanitarian law with a *teleology*, as if there was an in-built automatism in the idea of humanity and human rights that convinces states to comply through an inherent normative force (Florini 1996).

However, this is not the case, because norms require interpretation in a particular context (compare Wiener 2008; articles in Puetter and Wiener 2009; Kratochwil 2014). In IR, we cannot confine humanity to mean human rights only and explain its development with the sway of normativity. Ruti Teitel points out that the "meaning(s) of humanity law are [not entirely] controlled by such committed professionals [i.e. human rights lawyers and activists]" (Teitel 2011: 30). Because this is the case, meanings may change the discourse of international politics "sometimes in ways neither necessarily anticipated nor desired" (ibid.). In furthering the critique raised by critical constructivism to the treatment of norms as independent variables causing state behaviour, a focus on the hermeneutic embeddedness of "politics among people" is able to explain the development of transnational human and humanitarian relations through the topos of "Humanity". The following case study is merely a small piece of this puzzle. Nevertheless, it is possible to show that intervention did not occur as a result of the existence of the Universal Declaration of Human Rights but rather as a result of changes in people's horizons and hence of the play of performances.

In sum, I contend that the understanding of humanity is better developed among scholars of international law than among IR theorists. Humanity, and accordingly human rights, is part of politics among people in the sense discussed in the opening chapters relating to both the subject *and* a standard of treatment. The perspective of "Humanity" as a topos offers leverage for explaining the puzzle outlined at the beginning of the chapter. Because humanity has the aforementioned dual quality, I argue that it is a meta-narrative that helps understand certain actions such as the German participation in NATO intervention in Kosovo in 1999.

From pacifism to intervention

The trajectory of the Green Party reveals that some of the principles of "Humanity" were present since the beginnings of the party's formation. As part of the Greens' horizon, elements of humanity were central to the play of performances. As will become plain in the later sections, through the topos of "Humanity", it becomes possible to explain how the German foreign policy developed by the Social Democratic and Green coalition was the outcome of a development in which members of the party reconciled lessons from German history under the influence of an immediate confrontation with human suffering (Kundnani 2009; Brunstetter and Brunstetter 2011). Explaining the process through the topos of "Humanity" allows me to conclude that, at least in this case, global politics towards intervention was not the result of the alleged power of human rights in the UN General Assembly but rather the outcome of a widening of horizons.

Founding the Greens

The Greens were formally established as a party in 1980.[17] They originated from social movement groupings that had covered a wide spectrum of the political agenda across Germany since the late 1950s. These movements were usually single-issue initiatives which became increasingly active and visible during the subsequent decades. Founding members of the Greens originated from a background in grassroots initiatives as well as ecological movements, women's rights, and anti-nuclear campaigns (compare Volmer 1998: 22–23). Some had already been active participants in the Easter Marches against nuclear armament, as well as engaged in the student movements of the late 1960s (Scharf 1994: 2f.). Others were regulars at the so-called "Club Voltaires", local community centres with a distinctly alternative cultural agenda that can be characterised as left-liberal (Hockenos 2008). While none of this amounted to an orchestrated network of agenda-setting, the action of various social movements was contextualised, on the one hand, within a change in lifestyle marked by new attractions of consumerism and, on the other, by a heightening political engagement with war and violence in the present as well as in the past. Regarding the former, discontent was expressed against what appeared to be an overly materialistic culture, forms of authoritarianism, and patriarchy (Klein and Falter 2003: 16–23). Regarding the latter, particularly members of the student movements questioned the role of their parents' generation during the Nazi regime (Jarausch 2006). In its diversity, the Green Party contained anthropocentric as well as ecocentric traits (Eckersley 1992; Dobson 2007 [1990]), which did not, however, amount to a homogenous whole.

Against this background, the foundational consensus among a diverse set of members of the Green Party was a commitment to ecological reform (including the opposition to any type of nuclear technology), social justice, and grassroots democracy, as well as nonviolence.[18] As many commentators hold, it is possible to take as the unifying claim across this diverse set of agendas the title of one of Käthe Kollwitz's drawings, "Never again war" (Hyde-Price 2001; Zehfuss 2001; Stahl 2008; Brunstetter and Brunstetter 2011). The message of this dictum played a major role in the campaign to overcome the separation into military blocks in a bipolar world order. During the early days of the party, the overall consensus among members of the Greens was that Germany would leave NATO before long (Schnieder 1998: 88). In fact, once established, the party largely benefitted from an influx of members of the peace movement who were discontented with the German government's Social Democratic and Liberal coalition because of its support for the deployment of several hundred US missiles across Europe. Of these, around 200 Pershing II and Cruise missiles were to be stationed in Germany as part of NATO's "double-track" strategy, which was devised as a nuclear deterrent against a Soviet surplus of conventional forces.[19] Green activists, among the most prominent of whom were Petra Kelly and the former two-star General Gert Bastian, led rallies against this policy, at which an active engagement with the central claims of the 1960s mattered profoundly (Volmer 1998: 40f.). As Paul Hockenos summarises,

> The 1980s peace movement was led by a postwar generation that hadn't personally experienced war (many hadn't even experienced the 1960s) but appeared to have *internalized the lessons of Germany's recent past. They understood it as their moral imperative for Germans to stand up and oppose both their state and protector-mentor, the United States, on matters of military policy*. Quite remarkably, much of the country's younger generations, just four decades after Nazi rule and the Holocaust, seemed to be pacifists with an intensely critical relationship to nationalism and an unflinching inclination to question authority.
>
> (Hockenos 2008: 164, emphasis added)

Despite the engagement with the past and the concern for freedom and liberty as a common denominator in accordance with the topos of "Humanity", the Greens did not have a homogenous vision concerning how their aims should be achieved. Heated debates about the party's policies intensified as two opponent groups faced each other: the principled so-called "fundies" and the more pragmatic-leaning "realos" would quarrel about almost anything, from human rights issues to questions about the party's structure, and even held separate meetings (Longhurst 2004; Hockenos 2008: 215; Dryzek 2013 [1997]). By 1991, the realo wing appeared to be prevailing, and several prominent fundies left the party.

It is possible to argue that debates within the party reflect themes addressed by the topos of "Humanity" as outlined previously. For instance, Manon Maren-Grisebach, a founding member of the party, published a short book entitled *Philosophy of the Greens* in 1982 (orig. *Philosophie der Grünen*, notably without a definite or indefinite article in the title). She aims to specify the intellectual and ideological foundation of the party (Maren-Grisebach 1982: 7), addressing a range of themes which include human relations among each other in terms of power, peace, and equality, but also human relations towards nature as well as animals. Throughout the book, she interweaves policy proposals with references to philosophers, authors, scientists, and activists whose ideas she considers foundational to Green philosophy,[20] in order to highlight the broad basis of Green thinking. What is more, she emphasises themes of the topos of "Humanity", for instance, when addressing the themes of responsibility and compassion of humans towards each other as well as nature and animals, which speak to elements of equality, tolerance, and dignity but also of liberty (in particular with a view to women's rights and gender equality).

It was arguably not until a decade later that theoretical reflection explicitly linked *Green Political Theory* (Goodin 1992) with "Humanity", as Robert Goodin does in Chapter 2 of his book as well as several other passages throughout.[21] According to his reconstruction of Green politics, the emphasis lies on the themes of responsibility towards nature (Goodin 1992: 3) as well as fellow humans, as expressed in his Green Theory of Value in Chapter 2 but also in his remarks about a Green foreign policy marked by a respect for diversity (Goodin 1992: 199). Some of these aspects are shared in Robyn Eckersley's work on Green political theory, in which she emphasises new forms of representation and participation as well as relations among states and peoples (Eckersley 2004: 3), taking into account both environmental protection and questions of justice at home and abroad (ibid. 169). In her view, sovereignty should be reconceptualised (Eckersley 2005: 160f.), particularly in terms of outward-looking cosmopolitan norms of nationhood and citizenship (ibid. 176).

Green foreign policy during the 1990s

The topos of "Humanity" contains exactly such a broadened understanding of sovereignty and explains how the Greens came to accept the NATO mission in spring 1999. It enabled them to overcome their aversion and rejection of military means, which occasionally occurred grudgingly through argumentative exchange and at other times through physical experience and under emotional strain.

The concern about a revival of 1930s nationalism in the wake of German reunification (Probst 2007: 175) may have provided a common denominator among party members, as expressed in Kollwitz's dictum. Yet, despite the aforementioned apparent consolidation resulting from the departure of some of the party's founding members, regarding foreign policy making, there was nothing like an agreed-upon party line when the conflicts in Yugoslavia began. Throughout the 1990s, the Balkan War and the need to find a party position towards it brought the party under severe strain, and the organisation came close to breaking apart (Probst 2007: 182). While the Greens, in concert with the Social Democrats and the former German Democratic Republic-socialist party PDS (short for: Partei des Demokratischen Sozialismus/Party of Democratic Socialism),[22] had vehemently opposed the participation of German military personnel during the 1990–91 Gulf

War, the atrocities in the Balkans sparked a fierce debate among members, and the commitment to have Germany withdraw from NATO was still part of the electoral programme in the 1994 election. Although this particular commitment was dropped in 1998 (Klein and Falter 2003: 50), the Greens decided not to contribute to peace-making by military means and spoke out against an active engagement of the armed forces in conflicts during the 1998 electoral campaign, which eventually brought them into a coalition with the Social Democrats (Heinrich 2003: 28).

It is telling and supportive of the argument advanced here that the debate was no longer conducted among different wings of the party. Ultimately, the stance came down to individual decisions. Across the party, members saw themselves as confronted with a decision to choose between "never again war", that is, abstention from military intervention, and "never again Auschwitz", that is, being complicit in mass murder and ethnic cleansing by engaging in continuous rounds of peace negotiations that did not bring about the intended result (Hockenos 2008: 235–236). For example, while Joschka Fischer had opposed armed intervention in 1993, unlike his long-term friend and party ally Daniel Cohn-Bendit (Kundnani 2009: 239), two years later, his position changed after Serbian forces had occupied the town of Srebrenica in July 1995 and massacred approximately 7000 people. Fischer framed the event in the terms of Germany's Nazi past in a 12-page letter to the party dated 30 July 1995, which was also published in the newspaper *Die Tageszeitung*. He asks the question, "Doesn't the German left run the massive risk of tainting its soul when, regardless of the justification, ultimately it looks away from this new fascism? What becomes of our nonviolence when it bows to a kind of violence that takes human lives?"[23] Of course, the term "new fascism" is reminiscent of the lines of argument that had already marked the post-war generation's stance during the 1960s and is in accordance with "never again war". The phrase was likely to resonate with party members and the wider public, thereby giving credibility and conviction to the broader argument for the use of force.

However, even though his letter impressed some readers within the party and across Germany, the more hard-line pacifists remained unconvinced. Prominent party officials, namely Kerstin Müller, Claudia Roth, and Jürgen Trittin, responded in another public letter in which they accused Fischer of arguing for a duty of the United Nations to intervene.[24] Further, the then-speaker of the party, Ludger Volmer, suggested that Fischer take a gun and go to Sarajevo himself (Volmer 1998: 514; Hockenos 2008: 247). Winfried Nachtwei, one of the founding members of the Greens, recalls the position advanced during a meeting of the delegates of regional sections, where discontent stemmed from the following facts: first, arguably not all nonviolent means (including a petrol embargo) had been exhausted; second, the use of German forces might lead to a normalisation of out-of-territory missions for German foreign policy; and third, it could not be discounted that an intervention would not contribute to sparking further violence.[25] Particularly the latter two arguments are consistent with the "lessons learned" from WWII, namely that military force is an inappropriate tool of foreign policy, particularly given the German past. It also foreshadows Eckersley's contours of a "Green" understanding of sovereignty that calls for an emancipated representation rather than imposed decisions.

Nachtwei recalls that the Greens' delegates in the Bundestag were split over the question of whether Germany should support NATO's SFOR contingent, which had a UN mandate to oversee the Dayton Agreement.[26] Around 60% of the delegates voted against the mission, but the support of the other 40% was already seen as a positive result (Hockenos 2008: 249).[27] During the parliamentary debate on 6 December 1995, Joschka Fischer explicitly defended the Greens' decision not to support the government's plan to deploy troops to the contingent, recalling his position that the situation in Bosnia was marked by nationalism and a new fascism. At the same time, he acknowledged a conflict of values between nonviolence, on the one hand, and saving people's lives, on the other.[28] In the same debate, fellow Green MP Christa Nickels stated that nonviolent strategies had not been fully explored, opening her speech with an appeal to human civilisation: "Human civilization can only exist where those who act do so [. . .] especially in light of the suffering of living people, their hardships and where they are victims, and in the consciousness of lessons from history and with a view to the future".

While her position marks a first kindling of the compassion and dignity theme of "Humanity", a more complete turn-around was facilitated about a year later, even though it came at the cost of an intensified debate (Volmer 1998: 522). In October 1996, 18 delegates and high-ranking party officials travelled to Bosnia-Herzegovina to see and experience for themselves the impact and effects of the Balkan War.[29] Nachtwei recalls:

> Eventually we stood above Sarajevo and I later noted in my travel diary, "From the hillside above Serbian artillery, mortar shells and tanks were firing into the city as they pleased. Sarajevo [lay] on a plate, defenselessly trapped – for three years. Here it took me: grief and shame. Joschka [Fischer] teases Kerstin [Müller, then the party's spokeswoman of the members of parliament]: Surely custom officials would've been helpful here with their measurement sticks. [. . .] He later told me that he was ashamed to not have argued earlier for an intervention. He would never let this happen again." In this moment I experienced with brain and heart what happened. I inevitably took over the perspective of the victims. This was the same for the others. Later we had an audience with the Catholic bishop of Banja Luca, Franjo Komarica. He had a word with us that even the sturdiest of politicians had tears in their eyes. He reproached us with the charge, "What have you allowed to happen in a part of Europe again." Because with the exception of Austria the other European countries had not realized what had unfolded since the early 90s. They only did so once it was too late.[30]

This first-hand experience of the traumas of war made the delegation members change their outlook on the meaning of pacifism (see also Kundnani 2009: 240). In the previous quote, Nachtwei expresses how the experience and the bishop's accusation resonated with their memory of Nazi atrocities, as well as their personal moral sense of obligation that stemmed from that period of German history. The journey, which was the first of its kind by a German party delegation, induced a fusion of horizons that altered the party's overall stance through the reports that were drafted subsequently. For himself, Nachtwei recalls, "Never again must something like Srebrenica and Sarajevo happen under the auspices of European politics".[31]

This statement is a first indicator of a shifting position, a reconfiguration of the dictum "never again war". The direct confrontation with human suffering in Srebrenica broadened Nachtwei's, Fischer's, and others' outlooks on the use of force. For these members of the post-WWII generation, the absolute rejection of military means was superseded by a concern for the well-being of fellow humans. While it is possible to discern guidelines for future action that stem from the experience of the past, the path to achieve peace is no longer sought in exclusively peaceful ways. Nachtwei's horizon is readjusted in relation to a new context as it makes sense of events in Kosovo. As far as an active engagement in military conflict is concerned, he states,

> The *new insight* for me was that pacifism and nonviolence have to face up to the problem of how to deal with extremely illegal violence. There is a responsibility to protect (*Schutzverantwortung*). This responsibility to protect only marginally resides with an individual or a group. But in the context of public co-responsibility (*staatliche Mitverantwortung*) one cannot evade this question. Thus, nonviolence has to be framed in a different manner: nonviolence becomes the ultimate aim. Yet, while working towards that aim, one is responsible for controlling or limiting violence, for a nonviolent conflict solution as well as for the protection from illegal violence. Securing peace and the rule of law can necessitate the use of military forces in extreme cases, within the framework of the UN charter.[32]

The previous quote is indicative of a changed, broadened horizon which is expressed by the "new insight" as well as the fact that nonviolence has become an aim and no longer is considered the only means. In consequence, following the visit to Sarajevo in October, a year after the first debate on deploying German troops, during the parliamentary debate on 16 December 1996, Joschka Fischer demanded a UN-led contingent under Chapter VI [sic] to oversee the Dayton agreements.[33] While not supporting the government's proposal, the Greens were in favour of lending aid to the suffering. Angelika Beer, who was the party's spokesperson on defence policy at the time, foregrounded the theme of humanity in her speech during the same debate, stating that the people in Bosnia must not be forgotten merely because the Dayton Agreement had started a fragile peace process. She went on, "I cannot let that happen, because that would be similar to going into a hospital and stopping the drip of a seriously ill patient who I wish to survive".[34] Although they evoked compassion and the topos's element of dignity, Beer as well as Nachtwei in the previous quote express their new stance towards nonviolence. However, this does not mean that it had become a central component of the party's horizon just yet, as the following section shows.

The responsibility to intervene

While the visit to Bosnia and the subsequent discussion among the Greens had a considerable impact on their overall position towards military intervention, the issue was far from being settled. As the Balkan conflict reignited in the Kosovo region during the summer of 1998, so did the debate over the use of force among the Greens. They had just entered a coalition government with the Social Democrats, whose leaders had also been active protesters against the NATO two-track decision of the 1980s. Following the outbreak of violence in the Kosovo region, the Clinton administration in the United States considered the deployment of air strikes without the back-up of a UN resolution and requested support from their NATO allies. The soon-to-be Chancellor Schröder and Foreign Minister Fischer agreed (Baumann and Hellmann 2001: 75), as did the majority of the members of parliament who were summoned for an extraordinary session by still-acting Chancellor Kohl. Though some delegates of the Greens and Social Democrats voted against the support, most were in favour.

Despite NATO's threat to use military force, however, the atrocities continued. Negotiations in the French town of Rambouillet produced no positive result. Neither did a personal visit from Fischer to Serbian President Milosevic. On 24 March 1999, NATO began bombing targets in Serbia without a UN mandate. The contingent included aircraft from Germany, making this the first active German participation in military operations for 44 years.

Among the Greens, the ensuing discussion was considerably more heated than in other parties: "This was a crisis bigger and more threatening than any of the others the party had weathered over two decades" (Hockenos 2008: 268). Critics saw the bombings as the beginning of the normalisation of NATO deployment as a global police-force to justify its existence after the end of the Cold War – a view that is supported by research that emphasised that NATO changed its overall set-up during the Balkan crisis to include humanitarian missions in addition to "standard" military missions (Huysmans 2002).

In May 1999, the Green Party held an extraordinary party convention in the city of Bielefeld to allow more than 800 delegates to debate and vote on the matter of German involvement in the NATO bombings of Serbia. Again the importance of people's horizons came to the fore in the debate over the issue of whether nonviolence as a principle should trump a decision for involvement. However, as in the case of the delegation's visit to Bosnia in 1996, it is possible to detect a detachment from the sense of moral obligation stemming from the German past and which requires one to not engage in war, on the one hand, and a personal sense of obligation that may be loosely related to that past but which is dominated by a commitment to humanity, on the other. Paul Hockenos quotes the Green member of *Bundestag* Ursula Eid accordingly,

> The question we had to ask is whether the use of force is absolutely necessary in this case. Not: I'm against it because I'm a pacifist, because I'm German. Rather, what evidence speaks for the case that mass murder is happening or

genocide imminent that could be prevented? That's the question. This was a special case, under specific historical conditions, with no alternative.

(Hockenos 2008: 269)

It seems that many members of the Greens felt like Eid. During the heated party convention, at the beginning of which Foreign Minister Fischer was hit by a paint-filled balloon that broke his eardrum (Klein and Falter 2003: 63), delegate Sybille Haußmann supported the government's policy, stating that she was proud to have a Foreign Minister from the Green Party and that he should remain in office.[35] Foreign Minister Fischer took a more cynical position, answering his critics by saying, "Here is a war-monger talking to you, while you would perhaps like to suggest Mister Milosevic for obtaining the Nobel Prize for Peace".[36] Fischer's friend and former member of the European Parliament Daniel Cohn-Bendit restated his long-held position that it would amount to perversion to risk the lives of people in Kosovo for the sake of retaining the Greens' identity as a party of peace.[37]

These positions contrasted with those of the pacifist wing. For instance, Ulrich Cremer accused his party of committing a mistake of historic proportions because it would be responsible for aggression towards Yugoslavia. His position is still different from that of Kerstin Müller, who had been a delegation member during the trip to Sarajevo. She is quoted as having a bad conscience regardless of voting one way or other. Nevertheless, while she did not openly support the "realo" position towards the NATO engagement, she had moved some way from her argument expressed in the letter that she had co-authored in response to Fischer in 1995, when she had condemned any form of violence. In the end, 58% of the delegates, that is, a majority of 444 votes to 318, voted in support of the intervention and in particular of Fischer's position.[38]

Fischer had previously asked the Foreign Ministry to draft a peace plan that would include Russian diplomats and which foresaw the involvement of a UN-led peacekeeping mission. In brief, the plan initiated a multilateral consultation between European, US, and Russian envoys over the question of the post-war constellation in Kosovo, as well as negotiations with the Serbian leaders. NATO halted the air strikes on 10 June, after Milosevic signed the agreement on the previous day – that is, after ten weeks of bombings. From the German perspective, what is remarkable is that "it was the very parties that wrote pacifism and a non-militaristic foreign policy on their banners [. . .] that dared to shake the republic loose from its Bonn origins and pursue a course that would have an even greater impact on Germany's collective consciousness than their vaunted environmental and social reforms" (Henneke 2003, quoted in Hockenos 2008: 273).

Conclusion

A perspective that focuses on hermeneutic encounters and the politics among people shows that the practice of humanitarian intervention and the implementation of human rights does not spread across the globe on the basis of an inherent normative force. "Humanity", as the topos that explains German foreign policy at the turn of the millennium, had been an element of the Green horizon for some time, but its manifestation in action required considerable exposure to atrocities and debates among party members. As the reconstruction previously shows, the conviction that action was required did not come easily – neither for individuals, nor for the group as a whole.

At the same time, it would be misleading to conclude that a realisation of "Humanity" put the party's stance towards foreign policy, and indeed German foreign policy in general, on a path-dependent trajectory (see also Longhurst 2004). The Greens opposed the US-led campaign that eventually brought down Saddam Hussein in Iraq, and Germany, under the government of the Christian Democrats and the Liberal Party, abstained from voting on UN Security Council Resolution 1973 in 2011, which mentioned RtoP for the first time in conjunction with Chapter VII and the clause "to use all necessary means". Hence, contrary to recent enquiries into the *Persistent Power of Human Rights* which focus on how commitment to the norm can be turned into compliance (Risse and Ropp 2013: 5), it is possible to conclude that the "rules of the game" of foreign policy making are far from settled. The case study conducted in this chapter provides a different conclusion. Despite the existence of the Universal Declaration of Human Rights, the impetus for intervention did not come through the UN system. At least in this particular case, an important contribution to the eventual development of RtoP was enabled by hermeneutic encounters. It initially took place at the sub-state level, to use the parlance of the literature, but eventually *the very same people* rose to positions that allowed them to turn their normative convictions into German foreign policy. Hence, in the case of Germany, it was not a process of norm entrepreneurs creating the context for states to behave in a particular manner, and, subsequently, it did not put German foreign policy on a particular path for the future. While "Humanity" may have enabled the eventual position of the party, human agency allows for an open-ended play of performances so that future trajectories cannot be predicted from the past.

Beyond this added insight into IR, the case discussed in this chapter is an important normative contribution to the trajectory of global politics. I do not claim that the German Greens were centrally involved in the development of RtoP and humanitarian international law. What I have presented is but a small piece of the larger puzzle out of which RtoP eventually emerged and an answer to the question of how it was possible for Germany to participate in the NATO mission. Although it was in breach of international law, as it was carried out without a UN mandate (Lepard 2002; Wheeler 2002), what happened contributed to altering the meaning of sovereign statehood in international politics, which increasingly emphasised states' responsibility in terms of solidarity and compassion for their own citizens *and* for those of other countries (Glanville 2014; de Carvalho and Costa Lopez 2018). In a process of politics among people, the Greens posed ethical question about responsibility in the name of humanity and related questions of legitimate authority that would decide whether invasion was justified (Havercroft 2012).

Accordingly, this chapter has shown how a perspective that situates the locus of international politics in terms of politics among people may provide an answer to the puzzling question of the development and persistence of humanitarian intervention and human rights *and* how it was possible for Germany to participate in the mission despite its long-established identity as a passive member of NATO and despite any immediate material or security benefits. The development was a performative process in which people came to reconcile their horizon, allowing them to arrive at an ethical decision. This was not a simple and straightforward undertaking, as the discussion showed, because it went against the very ideals for which the Greens had campaigned for decades. However, as elements of the topos of "Humanity" had been present from the beginning, it was possible to re-interpret the German past and discover a forward-looking agenda that required taking action against the atrocities committed in the Balkans. To obtain this insight, it was important to introduce a process-oriented perspective based on hermeneutic concepts to the consistent and critical constructivist portfolio, as discussed in Chapter 3.

Notes

1 Parts of the empirical material and the argument presented in this chapter were previously published as Hansen-Magnusson (2014).
2 The International Commission on Intervention and State Sovereignty (ICISS) released a report on the Responsibility to Protect which offers an extensive discussion of state sovereignty in connection with the obligations of other states to intervene if a population suffers "serious harm as a result of internal war, insurgency, repression or state failure, and the state in question is unwilling or unable to halt or avert it" (ICISS 2001: XI). In these circumstances, "the principle of non-intervention yields to the international responsibility to protect" (ibid.). Occasionally the responsibility to protect is abbreviated as R2P. Concerning an overview of the historical development of RtoP, see Weiss (2007), Bellamy (2010), and Loges (2013). A critical position is advanced by Hehir (2012).
3 The operation lasted from 23 March to 10 June 1999. It began after peace talks between delegations from Yugoslavia and Kosovo in the French town of Rambouillet had broken down. The talks were meant to end clashes between Serbian and Kosovan armed forces which had begun in 1998. Information about the operation can be retrieved from NATO briefings available online: www.nato.int/kosovo/all-frce.htm [accessed 18 May 2019].
4 In contrast, Alex Bellamy argues that RtoP is not a norm as such, although parts of it are, and that its character has changed significantly since the ICISS report (Bellamy 2010).
5 The document S/RES/1973 (2011) is available online: www.undocs.org/S/RES/1973%20(2011) [accessed 18 May 2019]. It was passed with ten votes and five abstentions by China, Russia, Germany, Brazil, and India.
6 Along with Bundestag parliamentarians of the Liberal Party, Social Democrats and the Greens had pressed charges against the deployment of German troops outside the NATO area. On 12 July 1994, the German Federal Court decided that such a deployment would be in accordance with the Grundgesetz if it took place within systems of mutual security, that is, under a UN mandate or as part of a NATO mission. The decision has reference numbers 2 BvE 3/92, 2 BvE 5/93, 2 BvE 7/93, and 2 BvE 8/93. As the German Federal Court provides online access to decisions only since 1998, the details of the decision can be found online: www.servat.unibe.ch/dfr/bv090286.html [accessed 22 May 2019].
7 The treaty establishing NATO and its articles are available online: www.nato.int/cps/en/natolive/official_texts_17120.htm [accessed 18 May 2019].

8   While most commentators point out that the Green election manifestos included demands to withdraw from NATO, Volmer's discussion is more nuanced. As a founding member of the party, he argues that the Greens were striving for a change in the overall security architecture in Europe which would render NATO obsolete eventually; see Volmer (1998: 203ff. and 531ff.). I am aware that given Volmer's prominent status in the party, drawing extensively from his book might tip our account in a particular direction. Nevertheless, being aware of his role is a first step towards treating his account with due academic caution. Further, as it is based on his dissertation at the University of Bochum, it has undergone academic scrutiny, which is more than can be said for some of the other available sources on the Greens' trajectory and policies.
9   What I refer to as the "Balkan War" or the "Balkan crisis" in the context of this book is sometimes called the "Yugoslav (Civil) War" in order to distinguish the confrontations that led to the break-up of Yugoslavia during the 1990s from a war that was fought in the region in 1912/13.
10 While claiming to reconstruct Western European debates, Hansen's study mostly relies on sources from the United States (Chapter 6) and the United Kingdom (Chapter 7).
11 Holenstein points out that while the European Renaissance first developed in the cities of Northern Italy, the understanding of humanity could not have progressed without the influx of ideas from surrounding intellectual centres. Understandings of Roman law arrived there via Beirut and Constantinople, Hellenic philosophy via Cordoba, and Hindu-Arabic mathematics via the (Algerian) city of Béjaïa, while the idea that people are principally equal and free, which mattered in Early Modern times, is attributed to Ulpian of Tyros (Holenstein 2004: 114).
12 Grotius formulates rules of war, that is, jus ad bellum and jus in bello, which are meant to apply universally to all parties involved and at all times. Hence, despite potential causes for war, humans are equal in being human and should tolerate this trait.
13 Note that it is not my intention to provide an encompassing account of humanity across similar or different philosophical arguments. There are other potential references in the literature than the ones mentioned here. The point here is to highlight that humanity has been and remains a concern in the discussion.
14 Further developments and codifications can be found in references to laws of humanity that Turkey was accused of breaching after the massacres of Armenians in 1915; the Geneva Convention and Protocols of 1949, 1977, and 2005; the Nuremberg and Tokyo trials after WWII; the Charter of the United Nations; the International Criminal Tribunal for the former Yugoslavia (ICTY); and the International Criminal Tribunal for Rwanda (ICTR) (S/RES/827 (1993) and S/Res/955 (1994). For discussions of the development of humanitarian law, see Teitel (2011: 25–30) and Burke (2011: 102).
15 Where the public conscience is to be found and what it entails remains subject of debate among international law scholars.
16 Consider also the conceptual discussion by UN Secretary General Kofi Annan on "two concepts of sovereignty", in which he states that "humanity is indivisible" to support the argument that intervention may be warranted. The article was published in *The Economist* on 16 September 1999. It is available online: www.economist.com/node/324795 [accessed 28 October 2013].
17 The party was founded on 12/13 January 1980 in Karlsruhe (Klein and Falter 2003: 41).
18 This is not to say, though, that the overall outlook of the party was left leaning and progressive, nor that these attributes were uncontested. Quite the contrary; the party included national conservatives and spiritual-minded naturalists, among others, and could only barely agree on this set of principles that provided ample room for interpretation (Probst 2007: 174; Hockenos 2008: 149)
19 NATO's decision was taken on 12 December 1979. It offered the Warsaw Pact a mutual limitation of mid-range ballistic missiles while also allowing for a deployment of modernised mid-range nuclear weapons (Volmer 1998: 31).

20 These include Arthur Schopenhauer, Aristotle, Francis of Assisi, Laotse, Erasmus of Rotterdam, Paracelsus, Friedrich Hölderlin, Berthold Brecht, Berta von Suttner, Ernst Haeckel, Rosa Luxemburg, and Albert Schweitzer.
21 Taking the German Greens' manifesto as a central text of Green politics around the globe, Goodin mostly focuses on environmental issues but *does* link it to foreign policy and other policy areas.
22 The PDS has undergone a series of mergers with other parties. Since 2007, it has been called "Die Linke".
23 The letter to the party is archived and publicly available online: www.gruene.de/file admin/user_upload/Dokumente/Grüne_Geschichte/JoschkaFischer_Die_Katastrophe_in_Bosnien_und_die_Konsequenzen_fuer_unsere_Partei_1995.pdf [accessed 11 November 2011].
24 The authors of the response played prominent roles during the time of the coalition with the Social Democrats and are still at the party's top tier at the time of writing. The letter is also archived by the party and publicly available online: www.gruene.de/fileadmin/user_upload/Dokumente/Grüne_Geschichte/Wohin_fuehrt_die_Forderung_nach_einer_militaerischen_Interventionspflicht_gegen_Voelkermord.pdf [accessed 13 November 2011].
25 The interview is part of an archival project of the history of the Greens. It is available online: www.gruene.de/partei/30-gruene-jahre-30-gruene-geschichten/30-gruene-jahre-18-die-frage-der-militaerischen-gewalt.html [accessed 11 November 2011].
26 The Dayton Agreement was signed in Paris on 14 December 1995.
27 "Support", in this instance, is measured in contrast to negative votes: 2 members of the Greens voted in favour of the motion, while 16 abstained (Volmer 1998: 524).
28 The speech can be retrieved from the protocol of the debate in the Bundestag (protocol of the 76th session of the 13th parliamentary period) available online: http://dip21.bundestag.de/dip21/btp/13/13076.pdf [accessed 18 May 2019].
29 The journey took place between 20 and 25 October 1996 (Volmer 1998: 522).
30 The original source of this statement is available online: www.gruene.de/partei/30-gruene-jahre-30-gruene-geschichten/30-gruene-jahre-18-die-frage-der-militaerischen-gewalt.html [accessed 11 November 2011]. Nachtwei archived and re-published his travel log and notes on his personal website in 2016, available online: http://nachtwei.de/index.php?module=articles&func=display&aid=1431 [accessed 10 July 2019].
31 Available online: www.gruene.de/partei/30-gruene-jahre-30-gruene-geschichten/30-gruene-jahre-18-die-frage-der-militaerischen-gewalt.html [accessed 11 November 2011].
32 Ibid.
33 The protocol of the 149th session of the 13th parliamentary period is available online: http://dip21.bundestag.de/dip21/btp/13/13149.pdf [accessed 18 May 2019].
34 Ibid.
35 This citation is taken from the article "Die Machtfrage ist beantwortet" from *Berliner Zeitung* (14 May 1999) available online: www.berliner-zeitung.de/newsticker/die-basis-der-gruenen-ist-im-konsovo-konflikt-mehrheitlich-der-linie-des-parteivorstands-gefolgt–waehrend-die-spd-das-ergebnis-als-unterstuetzung-fuer-die-bundesregierung-wertet–kritisieren-cdu–fdp-und-pds-den-beschluss-als-widerspruechlich–die-machtfrage-ist-beantwortet,10917074,9638802.html [accessed 20 May 2019].
36 From the section "Worte der Woche", that is, quotations of the week, from *Die Zeit*, available online: www.zeit.de/1999/21/199921.wowos_zsp.xml [accessed 20 May 2019].
37 *Berliner Zeitung*, 14 May 1999, available online: www.berliner-zeitung.de/newsticker/die-basis-der-gruenen-ist-im-konsovo-konflikt-mehrheitlich-der-linie-des-parteivorstands-gefolgt–waehrend-die-spd-das-ergebnis-als-unterstuetzung-fuer-die-bundesregierung-wertet–kritisieren-cdu–fdp-und-pds-den-beschluss-als-widerspruechlich–die-machtfrage-ist-beantwortet,10917074,9638802.html [accessed 20 May 2019].
38 Ibid.

References

Aalberts, T. E. (2004). The Future of Sovereignty in Multilevel Governance Europe – A Constructivist Reading. *Journal of Common Market Studies* **42**(1): 23–46.
Bartelson, J. (1995). *A Genealogy of Sovereignty*. Cambridge, Cambridge University Press.
Baumann, R. and G. Hellmann (2001). Germany and the Use of Military Force: Total War, the Culture of Restrained and the Quest for Normality. *German Politics* **10**(1): 61–82.
Bellamy, A. J. (2010). The Responsibility to Protect – Five Years On. *Ethics & International Affairs* **24**(2): 143–169.
Berger, T. U. (1997). The Past in the Present: Historical Memory and German National Security Policy. *German Politics* **6**(1): 39–59.
Brunstetter, D. and S. Brunstetter (2011). Shades of Green: Engaged Pacifism, the Just War Tradition, and the German Greens. *International Relations* **25**(1): 65–84.
Burke, A. (2011). Humanity After Biopolitics. *Angelaki: Journal of the Theoretical Humanities* **16**(4): 101–114.
Cassese, A. (2000). The Martens Clause: Half a Loaf or Simply Pie in the Sky? *European Journal of Interantional Law* **11**(1): 187–216.
Chandler, D. (2001). The People-Centred Approach to Peace Operations: The New UN Agenda. *International Peacekeeping* **8**(1): 1–19.
Dalgaard-Nielsen, A. (2005). The Test of Strategic Culture: Germany, Pacifism and Pre-Emptive Strikes. *Security Dialogue* **36**(3): 339–359.
De Carvalho, B. and J. Costa Lopez (2018). The Emergence of Sovereignty: More Than a Question of Time. *International Studies Review* **20**(3): 489–494.
Dobson, A. (2007 [1990]). *Green Political Thought*. London and New York, Routledge.
Dryzek, J. S. (2013 [1997]). *The Politics of the Earth – Environmental Discourses*. Oxford, Oxford University Press.
Eckersley, R. (1992). *Environmentalism and Political Theory*. London, UCL Press.
Eckersley, R. (2004). *The Green State: Rethinking Democracy and Sovereignty*. Cambridge, MA, The MIT Press.
Eckersley, R. (2005). Greening the Nation-State: From Exclusive to Inclusive Sovereignty. *The State and the Global Ecological Crisis*. J. Barry and R. Eckersley. Cambridge, MA and London, The MIT Press: 159–180.
Finnemore, M. (1996b). Constructing Norms of Humanitarian Intervention. *The Culture of National Security*. P. Katzenstein. New York, Columbia University Press: 153–185.
Finnemore, M. and K. Sikkink (1998). International Norm Dynamics and Political Change. *International Organization* **52**(4): 887–917.
Florini, A. (1996). The Evolution of International Norms. *International Studies Quarterly* **40**: 363–389.
Geis, A. (2006). Den Krieg überdenken: Kriegsbegriffe und Kriegstheorien in der Kontroverse. *Den Krieg überdenken: Kriegsbegriffe und Kriegstheorien in der Kontroverse*. A. Geis. Baden-Baden, Nomos: 9–47.
Gholiagha, S. (2015). 'To Prevent Future Kosovos and Future Rwandas.' A Critical Constructivist View of the Responsibility to Protect. *The International Journal of Human Rights* **19**(8): 1074–1097.
Glanville, L. (2014). *Sovereignty and the Responsibility to Protect: A New History*. Chicago and London, The University of Chicago Press.
Goodin, R. E. (1992). *Green Political Theory*. Oxford, Polity Press.
Hansen, L. (2006). *Security as Practice: Discourse Analysis and the Bosnian War*. London, Routledge.

Hansen-Magnusson, H. (2014). Memory, Trauma and Changing International Norms – The German Green Party's Struggle with Violence and Its Quest for Humanity. *Memory and Trauma in International Relations – Theories, Cases and Debates*. E. Resende and D. Budryte. London, Routledge: 153–167.

Havercroft, J. (2012). Was Westphalia 'All That'? Hobbes, Bellarmine, and the Norm of Non-Intervention. *Global Constitutionalism* **1**(1): 120–140.

Hehir, A. (2012). *The Responsibility to Protect: Rhethoric, Reality, and the Future of Humanitarian Intervention*. Houndmills, Palgrave Macmillan.

Heinrich, G. (2003). *Bündnis 90/Die Grünen*. W. Woyke. Schwalbach, Wochenschau Verlag: 25–43.

Hockenos, P. (2008). *Joschka Fischer and the Making of the Berlin Republic: An Alternative History of Postwar Germany*. Oxford, Oxford University Press.

Holenstein, E. (2004). *Philosophie-Atlas: Orte und Wege des Denkens*. Zürich, Amman.

Huysmans, J. (2002). Shape-Shifting NATO: Humanitarian Action and the Kosovo Refugee Crisis. *Review of International Studies* **28**(3): 599–618.

Hyde-Price, A. (2001). Germany and the Kosovo War: Still a Civilian Power? *German Politics* **10**(1): 19–34.

International Commission on Intervention and State Sovereignty (ICISS) (2001). "The Responsibility to Protect." Report of the International Commission on Intervention and State Sovereignty http://www.iciss.ca/report-en.asp.

Jahn, B. (2000). *The Cultural Construction of International Relations*. Basingstoke and New York, Palgrave Macmillan.

Jarausch, K. H. (2006). Critical Memory and Civil Society: The Impact on the 1960s on German Debates about the Past. *Coping with the Nazi Past. West German debates on Nazism and Generational Conflict, 1955–1975*. P. Gassert and A. E. Steinweis, Eds. New York and Oxford, Berghahn Books: 11-30.

Klein, M. and J. W. Falter (2003). *Der lange Weg der Grünen: eine Partei zwischen Protest und Regierung*. München, Beck.

Kratochwil, F. (2014). *The Status of Law in World Society: Meditations on the Role and Rule of Law*. Cambridge and New York, Cambridge University Press.

Kundnani, H. (2009). *Utopia or Auschwitz – Germany's 1968 Generation and the Holocaust*. London, Hurst & Company.

Langenbacher, E. (2005). Moralpolitik Versus Moralpolitik: Recent Struggles over the Construction of Cultural Memory in Germany. *German Politics and Society* **23**(3): 106–134.

Lantis, J. (2002). The Moral Imperative of Force: The Evolution of German Strategic Culture in Kosovo. *Comparative Strategy* **21**(1): 21–46.

Lebow, R. N. (2009). Constitutive Causality: Imagined Spaces and Political Practices. *Millennium – Journal of International Relations* **38**(2): 211–239.

Leithner, A. (2009). *Shaping German Foreign Policy: History, Memory and National Interest*. Boulder, CO and London, First Forum Press.

Lepard, B. D. (2002). *Rethinking Humanitarian Intervention*. Philadelphia, Pennsylvania State University Press.

Loges, B. (2013). *Schutz als neue Norm in den internationalen Beziehungen: Der UN-Sicherheitsrat und die Etablierung der Responsibility to Protect*. Wiesbaden, Springer VS.

Longhurst, K. (2004). *Germany and the Use of Force*. Manchester and New York, Manchester University Press.

Maren-Grisebach, M. (1982). *Philosophie der Grünen*. München, Olzog.

May, L. (2005). *Crimes Against Humanity: A Normative Account*. Cambridge, Cambridge University Press.

Meron, T. (2000). The Martens Clause, Principles of Humanity, and Dictates of Public Conscience. *The American Journal of International Law* **94**(1): 78–89.

Milliken, J. and D. Sylvan (1996). Soft Bodies, Hard Targets, and Chic Theories: US Bombing Policy in Indochina. *Millennium: Journal of International Studies* **25**(2): 321–359.

Nabers, D. (2018). Towards International Relations Beyond the Mind. *Journal of International Political Theory*. https://doi.org/10.1177/1755088218812910.

Niemann, H. (2019). *The Justification of Responsibility in the UN Security Council*. Abingdon and New York, Routledge.

Peters, A. (2009). Humanity as the A and Omega of Sovereignty. *European Journal of International Law* **20**(3): 513–544.

Pradetto, A. (2006). The Polity of Germany Foreign Policy: Changes Since Unification. *Germany's Uncertain Power: Foreign Policy of the Berlin Republic*. H. W. Maull. Houndmills and New York, Palgrave Macmillan: 15–28.

Pradetto, A. (2014). Dekonstruktion von Souveränität: Diskurse zur Legitimierung militärischer Interventionen. *Die Friedens-Warte* **89**(3/4): 31–50.

Probst, L. (2007). Bündnis 90. *Handbuch der deutschen Parteien*. F. Decker and V. Neu. Wiesbaden, Verlag für Sozialwissenschaften: 170–188.

Puetter, U. and A. Wiener (2009). Contested Norms in International Relations. *Journal of International Law and International Relations* **5**(1).

Rathbun, B. C. (2004). *Partisan Interventions: European Party Politics and Peace Enforcement in the Balkans*. Ithaka, Cornell University Press.

Rathbun, B. C. (2006). The Myth of German Pacifism. *German Politics and Society* **24**(2): 68–81.

Reinhard, W. (1999). *Geschichte der Staatsgewalt: Eine vergleichende Verfassungsgeschichte Europas von den Anfängen bis zur Gegenwart*. München, C. H. Beck.

Rensmann, T. (2008). Die Humanisierung des Völkerrechts durch das ius in bello – Von der Marten'schen Klausel zur Responsibility to Protect. *Zeitschrift für ausländisches öffentliches Recht und Völkerrecht* **68**(1): 111–128.

Ringmar, E. (2018). The Problem with Performativity: Comments on the Contributions. *Journal of International Relations and Development*. Online First. https://doi.org/10.1057/s41268-018-0159-8.

Risse, T. and S. C. Ropp (2013). Introduction and Overview. *The Persistent Power of Human Rights. From Commitment to Compliance*. T. Risse, S. C. Ropp and K. Sikkink. Cambridge, Cambridge University Press: 3–23.

Risse, T., S. C. Ropp and K. Sikkink, Eds. (1999). *The Power of Human Rights: International Norms and Domestic Change*. Cambridge, Cambridge University Press.

Risse, T., S. C. Ropp and K. Sikkink, Eds. (2013). *The Persistent Power of Human Rights: From Commitment to Compliance*. Cambridge, Cambridge University Press.

Risse, T. and K. Sikkink (1999). The Socialization of International Human Rights Norms into Domestic Practices: Introduction. *The Power of Human Rights*. T. Risse, S. Ropp and K. Sikkink. Cambridge, Cambridge University Press: 1–38.

Ruggie, J. G. (1993). Territoriality and Beyond: Problematizing Modernity in International Relations. *International Organization* **47**(1): 139–174.

Scharf, T. (1994). *The German Greens: Challenging the Consensus*. Oxford, Berg.

Schnieder, F. (1998). *Von der sozialen Bewegung zur Institution? Die Entstehung der Partei DIE GRÜNEN in den Jahren 1978 bis 1980*. Münster, LIT Verlag.

Stahl, B. (2008). Nationale Geschichte(n) für den Krieg – der deutsche und französische Diskurs im Kosovo-Krieg und in der Irak-Krise. *Zeitschrift für Vergleichende Politikwissenschaft* **2**(2): 257–286.

Teitel, R. (2011). *Humanity's Law*. Oxford, Oxford University Press.
United Nations (1993). S/RES/827(1993). New York, available online: https://www.security councilreport.org/atf/cf/%7B65BFCF9B-6D27-4E9C-8CD3-CF6E4FF96FF9%7D/ IJ%20SRES827.pdf.
United Nations (1994). S/RES/955(1994). New York, available online: https://www.security councilreport.org/atf/cf/%7B65BFCF9B-6D27-4E9C-8CD3-CF6E4FF96FF9%7D/ IJ%20SRES955.pdf.
Volmer, L. (1998). *Die Grünen und die Außenpolitik – ein schwieriges Verhältnis: eine Ideen-, Programm- und Ereignisgeschichte grüner Außenpolitik*. Münster, Verlag Westfälisches Dampfboot.
Ward, I. (2003). *Justice, Humanity and the New World Order*. Burlington, Vermont, Ashgate.
Weiss, T. G. (2007). *Humanitarian Intervention: Ideas in Action*. Cambridge and Malden, MA, Polity Press.
Welsh, J. M. and M. Banda (2010). International Law and the Responsibility to Protect: Claryfing or Expanding State's Responsibility. *Global Responsibility to Protect* **2**(3): 213–231.
Wheeler, N. J. (2002). *Saving Strangers – Humanitarian Intervention in International Society*. Oxford and New York, Oxford University Press.
Wheeler, N. J. (2006). The Humanitarian Responsibility of Sovereignty: Explaining the Development of a New Norm of Military Intervention for Humanitarian Purposes in International Society. *Humanitarian Intervention and International Relations*. J. M. Welsh. Oxford and New York, Oxford University Press.
Wiener, A. (2008). *The Invisible Constitution of Politics: Contested Norms and International Encounters*. Cambridge, Cambridge University Press.
Wood-Donnelly, C. (2019). *Performing Arctic Sovereignty: Policy and Visual Narratives*. London and New York, Routledge.
Wüstenberg, J. (2017). *Civil Society and Memory in Postwar Germany*. Cambridge, Cambridge University Press.
Zehfuss, M. (2001). Constructivism and Identity: A Dangerous Liaison. *European Journal of International Relations* **7**(3): 315–348.
Zehfuss, M. (2007). *Wounds of Memory: The Politics of War in Germany*. Cambridge, Cambridge University Press.

6 Horizons of politics

How to deal with politics among people

Politics among People set out with two aims in mind. First, it aimed to develop a hermeneutic approach to global politics. I have argued that rather than taking place in the abstract, global politics takes place in encounters between people, and more attention needs to be paid to these encounters. The people may be the formal representatives of states, but the formal aspects of their meetings do not matter as much as the observation that it is the encounters between people that give meaning to global politics. People's horizons matter in these encounters, because it is on the basis of these that they make sense of the situation and engage in communicative practices of world-making, to paraphrase Onuf (1989).

This change of perspective on global politics is not an individualist approach in which what exists "in people's heads" takes centre stage, because the horizon is primarily social and cultural. As explained in Chapters 1 and 2, horizons and the prejudgements they entail are the results of embodied experience which are socially and culturally embedded. They make possible and shape the hermeneutic encounters that perpetuate global politics.

The second aim of the book was to build a consistent methodological approach that acknowledges the hermeneutic perspective. Somewhat ironically, hermeneutic scholarship has been sceptical of methods. For example, Gadamer (2004 [1975]) took exception primarily to the positivist approaches that had flourished since the 1960s. These approaches claimed to be able to conduct rigorous analysis of human behaviour, including politics, but, increasingly, they did so for the sake of demonstrating a method rather than working towards a particular end (Bernstein, Lebow et al. 2000: 44). However, interpretivism has come a long way towards demonstrating its merits concerning the understanding of global politics (Yanow and Schwartz-Shea 2013; Lynch 2014). If we adopt the premise that hermeneutic encounters shape global politics, it is consistent that we should address the double hermeneutic issue of interpreting others' interpretations and develop an approach that reflects this perspective.

The advantage of an interpretive approach is that it does not have to rely on unobservables (Puchala 1972, 2003), as does much of the mainstream of the discipline. Looking at how meaning is created and the ways in which it shapes global politics requires a perspective that relies on analysing actual practices of those involved. As specified in the opening chapters, many different ways of doing this have been developed, since more scholars have started to fully acknowledge that the world is socially constructed. *Politics among People* used their work as a springboard to specify how a hermeneutic perspective adds to our understanding of global politics and how such an approach translates into research.

The bottom line is that hermeneutic scholarship presents interpretation and meaning-making as a human condition. The debate about whether there are human universals and general structures that one can discern is ongoing (West 2007; Lebow 2008; Landmann 2012) and will not be resolved in this volume, and neither will the debate on the form and medium that meaning-making might privilege. International relations scholars have spent considerable time arguing whether language or discourse and ideas are separate from material factors (Laffey and Weldes 1997; Pouliot 2010; Schmidt 2010; Thakur 2011). Despite the recent surge in "new materialist" approaches (Lundborg and Vaughan-Williams 2015), *Politics among People* argues that meaning *must* take precedence over any material form. A case in point is Heidegger's discussion that a hammer is more than merely an object made of iron and wood. He argues that it needs to be understood in terms of its relations in space and time, including its use (2006 [1927]: 69).

Chapters 1 and 2 provided the groundwork for this approach. Rather than arguing about the workings of meaning-making and understanding in the abstract, it was argued that linguistics and psychology can and should inform how *Being* can be studied. Even though, as stated earlier, hermeneutic scholars have been sceptical of adopting natural science for all things social, it makes sense to try to incorporate research findings into the analyst's horizon. Not doing so would be inappropriate.

Hermeneutic encounters

Stating that global politics does not take place in the abstract, but actually in encounters between people, requires a closer look at these interactions and how they take place. The horizons of those involved inform what I called performances – that is, the practical instantiation of sense- and meaning-making. As memory studies have long argued, performance is based on and instantiates culture (Assmann 2006; Bevir and Rhodes 2010). In this light, the interpretivist groundwork I referred to in the opening two chapters has taken the study of global politics towards a distinctly cultural approach (Lapid and Kratochwil 1996), though this still seems to come as a surprise to some constructivists two decades later (Reus-Smit 2017).

Performances are based on the embodied understanding of one's surroundings, which is a social process. This understanding of language and meaning has been shown in research over the past two decades and appears to be currently the best available approximation of "how understanding works". Objects do not have meaning in themselves, as Heidegger and others have pointed out, which is why we should be cautious of privileging materialist understandings. Even though nature and technology have profoundly changed the context of human existence in the past decades (Latour and Porter 2017), what matters is how the context is perceived by those in it.

Performances and hermeneutic encounters may therefore come in a number of different forms. The use of objects may matter, but it is crucial how they are put into use and what kind of reciprocal relation they establish with others. That is to say, how other people engage with and make sense of the encounter matters. This perspective offers a range of access points for enquiry, starting with the individual perspective that may be retrieved from interviews and statements and moving to the more general social interaction of conference proceedings and drafts of convention texts that one can observe and seek to interpret.

Hermeneutic methodology

Being is inseparable from world-making, and of course it is not confined to hermeneutic encounters as objects of study. The researcher is also part of a web of meaning-making and is necessarily applying his or her own perspective in the analysis – comprising embodied experience as well as socially and culturally mediated knowledge. This double hermeneutic contrasts with the detached approach advanced by positivists. The latter has been thoroughly debunked during the so-called Third Debate in International Relations (Wæver 1996). (However, the lack of response by positivist scholars makes it questionable to what extent such a debate actually ever properly took place.)

Hermeneutic methodology has to account for these double hermeneutics, and Chapter 3 suggested a number of criteria according to which the interpretation of others' interpretations could proceed. The aim of following these criteria is to create a broader sense of transparency and make the analytical processes more comprehensible. In addition, *Politics among People* built its analysis around the concept of topos as a narrative device for making sense of one's observations. Topoi are not dissimilar to what has been referred to as "basic concepts" (Guzzini 2013; Berenskoetter 2017), but they are more complex because they are a narrative bundle that emerges from interpreting one's object of study. The aim of a topos is building a theory with regard to particular problems or analytical issues – not in the sense of a grand theory of the social world, but suggesting that we can understand and explain particular phenomena when taking into account a set of issues surrounding the hermeneutic encounters we observe and their context.

The abductive procedure creates a mid-level account that follows the same parameters for understanding knowledge in the hermeneutic sense more broadly, that is, that one's horizon may be subject to change over time. In this regard, academic knowledge is similarly subject to revision. Topoi are not so much the final answer but rather the beginning and part of a continuous conversation.

The cases

In this light, the analyses in the empirical chapters of this book contribute to different conversations on contemporary issues in global politics. They concern the role and design of global institutions as well as the core categories of international relations theory.

The first case looked at the UN Convention on the Law of the Sea. It explained its trajectory and problematised its current working with regard to the topos of "Humanity". This conversation-starter problematises how governance institutions work and how they could work better in a normative sense, rather than a functional one (Wiener 2018; Zürn 2018). Expertise and technocratic solutions may be quick fixes to controversial issues, but they should not be ends in themselves. Rather, as a close look at the trajectory of the institutional set-up of the Law of the Sea shows, reflexivity needs to be accommodated in institutional design. This is to say that new knowledge of the operational environment of the organisations and of the broader context needs to be included.

As we can see from the example of the UN system in general, it appeared to be a sensible solution in the aftermath of WWII, but the procedural rules of the UN Security Council with its five veto powers are subject to extensive criticism nowadays, as they no longer command the legitimacy they did some 70 years ago. As with oceans and questions over access to resources, understandings of fairness and justice are not universal and timeless. Climate change is altering some of the parameters of the activities in the oceans with regard to fishing as well as shipping: fish stock move with warming waters (Pinsky, Reygondeau et al. 2018), and the loss of sea ice opens up new shipping lanes (Hansen-Magnusson 2019), while the protection of biodiversity in areas beyond national jurisdiction poses problems that UNCLOS had not anticipated (Tiller and Nyman 2018). Science is not a neutral arbiter, even though some laud science diplomacy as a general solution for governance issues (Berkman, Kullerud et al. 2017). When designing institutions, one needs to be aware that there is a relation between what one identifies as a problem in the first place and the solutions one proposes as a result (Jasanoff 2005). Horizons matter, so to speak, and their differences need accommodating. Just as science is not neutral, neither is law (Hansen-Magnusson, Vetterlein et al. 2018), which is why reflexive institutions are ever more important to adjust to changing circumstances and thereby increase the legitimacy of global governance.

The second case that *Politics among People* analysed shows that major categories of global politics, such as sovereignty, do not change easily. The case also highlights that one should be careful to attribute norms, such as human rights, with an innate power; this explains their proliferation since WWII (Risse, Ropp et al. 1999, 2013). Rather, one needs to look at hermeneutic encounters in order to be able to understand and explain how perceptions of sovereignty change over time and how norms such as human rights matter in the process of foreign policy making, for example.

Policy decisions are based on actors' horizons. Decisions may not fully explained by reference to functional calculations alone but rather involve ethics (Frost 2013; Gaskarth 2013). As the second case study shows, there was no imminent threat to survival that caused NATO to engage in the war in former Yugoslavia, just as the conflict did not pose an existential threat to Germany. What is more, participating in NATO missions posed a huge legitimacy challenge to the parties involved. How the Green Party struggled to understand what the war in former Yugoslavia stood for and what actions should be taken was part of a process of reconciliation involving the ethics of individual party members as well as the group more broadly. These ethics of decision-making can amount to a difficult personal choice. The struggles that were documented in the study show how horizons do not change on a whim, but they *may* do so, for example, as a result of embodied experience or following a reconsideration of what human rights mean in practice and how one should enact them.

While this insight pushes back against the view that actors decide based on utility and functional considerations, the case also underscores how an abstract focus on "national interests" seems to bear only small fruit (Weldes 1999) where it omits the impact of hermeneutic encounters. As the trajectory of German foreign policy shows, later decisions were not path dependent: the Social Democratic-Green Party coalition defended its decision not to join the United States and the United Kingdom in the 2003 Iraq war, even though the conservative opposition decried the loss of standing as a reliable partner – only to remain neutral with regard to participating in UNSC resolution 1973 in 2011. Foreign policy does not take place in a vacuum; rather, it relates to the ethics of those who make decisions and is part of a broader hermeneutic web.

Reflection

The focus on hermeneutic situations as the sites and ways in which global politics takes place may require some getting used to. It may leave readers with a number of questions concerning the outcomes of the case studies and the broader methodology, which is why I seek to address some of these questions towards the end of the book. These questions concern some of the possible limitations of focusing on a micro level of analysis, the universe of cases from which studies were pursued, the role of hermeneutic scholars upon whom the theoretical sections rely, the use of hermeneutic concepts more generally, and the question of the amount of material used for the case studies.

First, treating international relations as politics among people requires researchers to "go micro" (Checkel 1998; Adler 2002). Therefore, the question would be whether approaching international relations as politics among people loses the potential to address "macro" issues of global politics.

To address this question, it is worth reminding ourselves what "going micro" actually refers to. *Politics among People* was not the first work in IR to "go micro" in suggesting a hermeneutic conception of Being that emphasises processes of understanding. Going micro is a feature of interpretive research (Niemann and Schillinger 2017), but rational choice approaches do so, too. "Micro" in the context of this book meant a focus on people rather than states or other unobservables, which are often taken as the constitutive units of the system of international politics. In any case, the focus on people and hermeneutic encounters is not an individualist approach but rather one that considers people as embedded in a social and cultural web. The advantage, it is argued, lies in moving IR away from studying abstract entities, because doing so enables research to address how politics takes place and through whom. This approach borrows from anthropology, as discussed in Chapters 2 and 3 (Shore 2000; Neumann 2012), and avoids having to rely on abstract concepts. As our operationalisation through the concept of "topos" showed, valuable insights can be derived regarding questions of contemporary global politics which cannot be answered by a focus on unobservables.

A second question that may arise concerns what is conventionally known as the "universe of cases". Often "states" or "organisations" are used to structure the object of study – for instance, the emergence of global human rights. Typically, research compares the object of study with regard to two or more constitutive units or engages in an in-depth discussion of a particular unit whose selection is carefully argued (often because studying the unit allows for representative conclusions about a broader phenomenon).

Of course, *Politics among People* also operated with a universe of cases in that it concerned theories of IR – in Chapters 1 and 2 – and examples of normative developments that matter for contemporary global governance. As discussed in Chapters 2 and 3, focusing on hermeneutic encounters may be a virtue in that it becomes possible to address human agency as the underlying cause of developments. In this regard, the book helps to expand the "universe of cases" because it may be possible to detect pockets of the universe that would be hidden from view for research relying on unobservables. It strengthens the argument made by disciplines other than IR over a number of years, that is, that research should move beyond "methodological nationalism" and devise new theories of IR (Zürn 2013: 417). Hence, approaching international relations as politics among people offers a first step towards rethinking global politics.

A third issue may result from the predominant reliance on the work of Hans-Georg Gadamer and Paul Ricœur rather than on other authors to advance constructivist approaches to IR and hermeneutics for our operationalisation. Perhaps drawing on another author would have led to different results? Of course, Gadamer and Ricœur are not the only hermeneutic scholars. The works of Cambridge School scholars like Quentin Skinner or James Tully, as well as the work of Charles Taylor, could have proven a fruitful addition (Tully 1988). However, at this point, it was simply beyond the scope of the book to integrate concepts from all other potential sources. Gadamer and Ricœur seemed like a good choice because references to their work have been part of the debate among critical constructivists for two decades (Neufeld 1993; Kornprobst 2013), but they had not been operationalised for empirical work, which might be increasingly necessary in the future (Juntunen 2013). Regarding IR theory, Gadamer's concepts also allowed the development of a complementary account to the legacy of Wittgenstein, from which most consistent constructivists draw, in order to focus on processes of world-making (Fierke 2002; Grimmel and Hellmann 2019). Of course, critics are correct to point out that Gadamer and Ricœur have little to say about social theory and, by implication, very little about research methodology. In fact, *Truth and Method* and *Memory, History, Forgetting* are critical of the latter. I concede that point of critique. Nonetheless, it was important to draw on hermeneutics in order to develop a perspective that focuses on the *processes* by which people draw on and create meanings and thereby shape the trajectory of politics. For this reason, it was necessary to move beyond Gadamer's and Ricœur's hermeneutics and draw on recent debates in interpretive social sciences for operationalising the empirical parts of the study.

A fourth set of questions relates to the use of hermeneutic concepts more generally. Is it not possible that the approach is blind to some aspects that it seeks to analyse? And, related to this question, is it not possible that the way the approach was operationalised for an interpretive study yields "only" subjective insights? Regarding the first question, this may well be true. However, it is also true of other theories, and it is in fact the nature of *theory* to be an abstraction from *reality*. Therefore, they cannot be the same. Just as a map is a different scale to the reality it seeks to capture, theory is a translation of reality in order to make the latter comprehensible. I would also argue that it is a trait of knowledge never to reach completion because horizons are subject to continuous fusion. The book *did* show, however, that it is possible to identify particular problems and successfully engage in theory-building through topoi in order to explain what is happening. In this regard, it is a virtue of a hermeneutic approach that it is not a full-scale social theory, because it allows us to use categories reflexively. Using topoi to understand and explain phenomena is a mid-range approach to global politics.

On this basis, regarding the second question, the method presented in Chapter 3 self-consciously requires the use of heuristics that guide the process of analysis. This procedure has been successfully used in empirical studies (Kruse 2011), and it ensures that others using that method should arrive at similar conclusions. Objectivism is a myth, just as myths have been built concerning subjectivist approaches, such as the notions that meanings are private and understanding is unstructured and without a natural basis. By contrast, the experience-based approach to understanding presented in this book – encapsulated by metaphors, for example – holds that there is a general structure to one's experience that is grounded in the ways in which people bodily interact in their environment (Lakoff and Johnson 1980: 224). Lakoff and Johnson argue that "[t]ruth is always relative to understanding, which is based on a nonuniversal conceptual system" (ibid. 226–227) but is also based on interactional properties that hold that meaning "always is meaning *to* a person", while the imaginative use of metaphors makes it possible "to give experience new meaning and to create new realities" (ibid. 228).

A final question might arise with regard to the number of sources and the amount of material used for the case studies. Of course, it is always possible to draw on additional data. In both cases, narrative interviews might have provided additional material from which new insights could have been derived, but constraints of time and budget prevented the collection of additional data. As much as I already drew on statements, including interviews printed in books or newspapers, conducting biographical interviews typical of "oral history" accounts (Ritchie 2011) remains a desideratum for further research on both empirical cases. Time is pressing, particularly regarding the early days of UNCLOS, as the memories of the remaining participants of the conference will surely fade. Perhaps their accounts will prove insightful beyond what was concluded already and may change people's horizons about these particular processes of contemporary global governance. In the meantime, it is possible to continue with the conclusions derived from the studies, as I will discuss in the following section.

Towards new horizons

Politics among People does not aspire to be a grand theory of IR, which scholars from across the spectrum of positions have recently declared undesirable anyway (compare the 2013 Special Issue of the *European Journal of International Relations*).[1] This book has engaged in different ways of problem-oriented theory-building at a mid level. In terms of the initial theoretical problem, it contributed to a particular strand of IR theory. The generalisability of the approach was demonstrated in the application to the case studies in Chapters 4 and 5. Both cases were puzzling in their own right and warranted an approach of "politics among people". It could be shown that new insights could be generated for both, as discussed previously, without claiming to have found new general laws of global politics. As stated earlier, critical constructivists have long since brought forward arguments against attempts to detect universal laws in social interaction. To paraphrase Friedrich Kratochwil (1993), no such laws have been detected, yet the vocabulary and methodology of nomothetic-deductive research continue to occupy a prominent position in IR. For this reason, the primary contribution of *Politics among People* addresses specific theoretical and empirical areas, rather than a general theory of global politics.

In the final paragraphs, I would like to sketch three avenues for further research. They concern: first, an engagement of hermeneutics with political theory in the context of global governance; second, outer space, a particular issue of global governance to which the hermeneutic framework could be applied; and third, foreign policy analysis more generally.

Concerning the involvement with political theory as a first avenue, approaching international relations as politics among people offers *one* way of considering processes that matter for contemporary global governance, while the open-ended nature of knowledge in the hermeneutic understanding entails that insights will be superseded eventually. Even though he insists on using unobservables to discuss global politics, Michael Zürn's recent discussion of global governance concludes with a number of observations that build bridges to more constructivist approaches, which might open the analyses for a stronger focus on micro-level interaction and meaning-making in epistemic or reflexive authorities (Zürn 2018: 264f.). This marks a convenient access point for hermeneutic theory to venture forward into theories of politics. Such research would then be able to discuss normativity and the underlying moral principles that shape relations between those who are engaged in a hermeneutic encounter. Normative political theory may be used as heuristic guidance in this context, as it has identified the "right to justification" (Forst 2012) or "access to contestation" (Wiener 2014) as structural principles that are supposed to raise the quality and legitimacy of relations between actors in global politics. However, it should not be forgotten that a hermeneutic "willingness to listen" (Dallmayr 1993; Roy and Starosta 2001) constitutes a prerequisite for any form of interaction that is supposed to improve legitimacy, as does a "capacity to participate". The latter is strikingly demonstrated during international negotiations where the sizes of the delegations from states and non-state actors vary widely. As discussions often take place in different forums simultaneously, less capable delegations cannot fully participate – but even in relatively small forums, capacity is polymorphic and displays considerable differentials (Tallberg 2008).

A second avenue for further refinement arises from the conclusions of the empirical analyses. For example, concerning the topos of "Comtean Positivism", the insights may be used to discuss issues of institutional design in contemporary ocean governance. Alternatively, because it follows from the conclusion that humanity is sidelined as a result of expertocracy and objectivity, this insight may be used as hypothesis for enquiries into other sectors of governance which are also meant to benefit humankind at large.

An obvious candidate for an enquiry such as this is Space Law, which has been developed by the UN Committee on the Peaceful Use of Outer Space (COPUOS), and in which interest has been surging in recent years (Hansen-Magnusson, Vetterlein et al. 2018; Sutch and Roberts 2019). COPUOS was created in 1959, a couple of years after the Soviet Union launched the Sputnik satellite, following the adoption of Resolution 1348 (XIII) in 1958.[2] Aided by an office, it is meant to enable cooperation in the peaceful use of outer space.[3] While the Committee has existed for more than five decades, parallels can be drawn to contemporary ocean governance in the fact that a heightened interest in space has been discernible in recent years. Like the Russian flag at the North Pole in August 2007 (Dodds 2010), India landed an unmanned spacecraft called Chandrayaan 1 on the moon in November 2008 and celebrated the fact that its flag had been set up on the lunar surface. Some five years later, China successfully landed an unmanned robotic rover on the moon.[4]

Further parallels with the current race to ownership in the Arctic are that the material gains from these lunar missions are difficult to quantify (Keil 2014; Hansen-Magnusson 2018). While the so-called Moon Treaty of 1979 states that the international community has jurisdiction over the moon, it has not been signed by any nation engaged in space flight.[5] Aside from this unresolved issue, a more pressing concern is that of available space for satellites in orbit around the Earth. Geostationary satellites must be located about 35000 km above the equator, but the room available for them is finite. As a solution, and to ensure that technologically advanced nations do not monopolise the available space, it could be possible to extend principles of UNCLOS to outer space. However, whether this is possible or, indeed, following the discussion in this book, *desirable* must be subject to further research and debate.

A third way to take hermeneutic research further builds upon the other empirical case. The topos of "Humanity" enabled an explanation for the German participation during the early days of humanitarian interventions, suggesting a number of possible future trajectories for research. For one, research could compare the foreign policy of other states that have a similar background to Germany regarding WWII. Japan is the obvious example, and indeed Peter Katzenstein has enquired into the Japanese culture of national security in the mid-1990s (1996). Given that Katzenstein identified nonviolent foreign policy at that time as resulting from institutionalised social and legal norms, about two decades later, in light of recent competitive claims with China to the Senkaku/ Diaoyu islands (Wirth 2017), it might be worth investigating how nonviolent foreign policy is sustained (or not) and how "Humanity" matters in this regard (or not).

Another perhaps more obvious follow-up study to the one presented in Chapter 5 would be to investigate German non-participation in the US-led mission in Libya in 2011. This instance raises new questions about German foreign policy and the development of intervention in global politics. At the time of this decision, Germany had a new government consisting of a coalition between the Christian Democrats and the Liberal party, of which the latter was in charge of the Foreign Ministry. The mission in Libya was backed by a Security Council resolution under Chapter VII which for the first time explicitly referred to RtoP and used the expression "all necessary means". Perhaps "Humanity" as a topos of German foreign policy is only applicable to the particular constellation at the late 1990s? Will it matter again one day if the Green Party returns to take charge of charge of foreign policy? Or does "Humanity" matter elsewhere in the presence or absence of a comparable party? For these lines of comparative enquiry, the study presented in Chapter 5 provides a necessary working hypothesis, while the framework laid out in Chapters 2 and 3 could guide the theoretical part.

Last, while the empirical analyses both touch upon contemporary problems of global governance, the first leaning towards international law and the second towards foreign policy analysis, it is possible to address politics among people in other empirical settings. Because *Politics among People* focuses on embedded agency and does not rely on "unobservables", where one ventures to investigate performances is a matter for the researcher's interests and ability to identify particular problems worthy of investigation. Furthermore, to a certain extent, it is also a matter of researchers being willing to expand their horizon to peer beyond conventional categories of international relations.

Notes

1 Compare especially contributions by Chris Brown and David Lake, who discuss the end of grand theory approaches (Brown 2013; Lake 2013).
2 The resolution on the "Question of the Peaceful Use of Outer Space" is available online: www.unoosa.org/pdf/gares/ARES_13_1348E.pdf [accessed 19 June 2019].
3 The United Nations Office for Outer Space Affairs (UNOOSA) is situated in Vienna.
4 Compare available online: http://news.bbc.co.uk/2/hi/south_asia/7730157.stm and www.bbc.co.uk/news/science-environment-25356603 [accessed 19 June 2019].
5 The treaty (RES 34/68) is available online: www.unoosa.org/pdf/gares/ARES_34_68E.pdf [accessed 19 June 2019].

References

Adler, E. (2002). Constructivism in International Relations. *Handbook of International Relations*. W. Carlsnaes, T. Risse and B. A. SImmons. London, Sage: 95–117.

Assmann, A. (2006). Memory, Individual and Collective. *The Oxford Handbook of Contextual Political Analysis*. R. E. Goodin and C. Tilly. Oxford, Oxford University Press: 210–224.

Berenskoetter, F. (2017). Approaches to Concept Analysis. *Millenium Journal of International Studies* **45**(2): 151–173.

Berkman, P. A., L. Kullerud, A. Pope, A. N. Vylegzhanin and O. R. Young (2017). The Arctic Science Agreement Propels Science Diplomacy. *Science* **358**(6363): 596–598.

Bernstein, S., R. N. Lebow, J. Gross Stein and S. Weber (2000). God Gave Physics the Easy Problems: Adapting Social Science to an Unpredictable World. *European Journal of International Relations* **6**(1): 43–76.

Bevir, M. and R. A. W. Rhodes (2010). *The State as Cultural Practice*. Oxford, Oxford University Press.

Brown, C. (2013). The Poverty of Grand Theory. *European Journal of International Relations* **19**(3): 483–497.

Checkel, J. T. (1998). The Constructivist Turn in International Relations Theory. *World Politics* **50**(2): 324–348.

Dallmayr, F. (1993). Self and Other: Gadamer and the Hermeneutics of Difference. *Yale Journal of Law and the Humanities* **5**(2): 507–529.

Dodds, K. (2010). Flag Planting and Finger Pointing: The Law of the Sea, the Arctic and the Political Geographies of the Outer Continental Shelf. *Political Geography* **29**(2): 63–73.

Fierke, K. M. (2002). Links Across the Abyss: Language and Logic in International Relations. *International Studies Quarterly* **46**(3): 331–354.

Forst, R. (2012). *The Right to Justification. Elements of a Constructivist Theory of Justice*. New York, Columbia University Press.

Frost, M. (2013). Middle Ground Ethics and Human Rights in International Relations. *Ethical Reasoning in International Affairs: Arguments from the Middle Ground*. C. Navari. Basingstoke, Palgrave Macmillan: 64–80.

Gadamer, H-G. (2004 [1975]). *Truth and Method*. New York, Continuum.

Gaskarth, J. (2013). Interpreting Ethical Foreign Policy: Traditions and Dilemmas for Policymakers. *British Journal of Politics and International Relations* **15**(2): 191–209.

Grimmel, A. and G. Hellmann (2019). Theory Must Not Go on Holiday. Wittgenstein, the Pragmatists, and the Idea of Social Science. *International Political Sociology* **13**(2): 198–214.

Guzzini, S. (2013). The Ends of International Relations Theory: Stages of Reflexivity and Modes of Theorizing. *European Journal of International Relations* **19**(3): 521–541.

Hansen-Magnusson, H. (2018). Arctic Geopoetics: Russian Politics at the North Pole. *Cooperation and Conflict*. https://doi.org/10.1177/0010836718815526.

Hansen-Magnusson, H. (2019). The Web of Responsibility in and for the Arctic. *Cambridge Review of International Affairs*. https://doi.org/10.1080/09557571.2019.1573805.

Hansen-Magnusson, H., A. Vetterlein and A. Wiener (2018). The Problem of Non-Compliance: Knowledge Gaps and Moments of Contestation in Global Governance. *Journal of International Relations and Development*. https://doi.org/10.1057/s41268-018-0157-x.

Heidegger, M. (2006 [1927]). *Sein und Zeit*. Tübingen, Max Niemeyer.

Jasanoff, S., Ed. (2005). *States of Knowledge: The Co-Production of Science and Social Order*. London, Routledge.

Juntunen, T. (2013). How Does History Work (In) Our Perceptions and Practices? Hans-Georg Gadamer's Philosophical Hermeneutics and the 'Practice Turn' in IR. *Paper Presented at the 8th Pan-European Conference on International Relations, University of Warsaw, Poland (18–21 September 2013)* [on file with the author].

Katzenstein, P. J. (1996). *Cultural Norms and National Security: Police and Military in Postwar Japan*. Ithaca, NY, Cornell University Press.

Keil, K. (2014). The Arctic: A New Region of Conflict? The Case of Oil and Gas. *Cooperation and Conflict* **49**(2): 162–190.

Kornprobst, M. (2013). When the Discipline Is Not Enough – Scholarship, Communication Power. *Paper Prepared for Presentation at the 8th International Interpretive Policy Analysis Conference (IPA) in Vienna (3–5 July 2013)* [on file with the author].

Kratochwil, F. (1993). The Embarrassment of Changes: Neorealism as the Science of Realpolitik Without Politics. *Review of International Studies* **19**(1): 63–80.

Kruse, J. (2011). *Reader 'Einführung in die Qualitative Interviewforschung'*. Freiburg available online: www.qualitative-workshops.de.

Laffey, M. and J. Weldes (1997). Beyond Belief: Ideas and Symbolic Technologies in the Study of International Relations. *European Journal of International Relations* **3**(2): 193–237.

Lake, D. A. (2013). Theory Is Dead, Long Live Theory: The End of the Great Debates and the Rise of Eclecticism in International Relations. *European Journal of International Relations* **19**(3): 567–587.

Lakoff, G. and M. Johnson (1980). *Metaphors We Live By*. Chicago and London, University of Chicago Press.

Landmann, T. (2012). Phronesis and Narrative Analysis. *Real Social Science – Applied Phronesis*. B. Flyvbjerg, T. Landmann and S. Schram. Cambridge, Cambridge University Press: 27–47.

Lapid, Y. and F. Kratochwil (1996). *The Return of Culture and Identity in IR Theory*. Boulder, CO, Lynne Rienner.

Latour, B. and C. Porter (2017). *Facing Gaia: Eight Lectures on the New Climatic Regime*. Cambridge, UK and Medford, MA, Polity Press.

Lebow, R. N. (2008). *A Cultural Theory of International Relations*. Cambridge, Cambridge University Press.

Lundborg, T. and N. Vaughan-Williams (2015). New Materialisms, Discourse Analysis, and International Relations: A Radical Intertextual Approach. *Review of International Studies* **41**(1): 3–25.

Lynch, C. (2014). *Interpreting International Relations*. New York and London, Routledge.

Neufeld, M. (1993). Interpretation and the 'Science' of International Relations. *Review of International Studies* **19**(1): 39–61.

Neumann, I. B. (2012). *At Home with the Diplomats: Inside a European Foreign Ministry*. New York, Cornell University Press.

Niemann, H. and H. Schillinger (2017). Contestation 'All the Way Down'? The Grammar of Contestation in Norm Research. *Review of International Studies* **43**(1): 29–49.

Onuf, N. (1989). *World of Our Making: Rules and Rule in Social Theory and International Relations*. Columbia, University of South Carolina Press.

Pinsky, M. L., G. Reygondeau, R. Caddell, J. Palacios-Abrantes, J. Spijkers and W. W. L. Cheung (2018). Preparing Ocean Governance for Species on the Move – Policy Must Anticipate Conflict over Geographic Shifts. *Science* **360**(6394): 1189–1191.

Pouliot, V. (2010). *International Security in Practice: The Politics of NATO-Russia Diplomacy*. Cambridge, Cambridge University Press.

Puchala, D. (1972). Of Blind Men, Elephants, and International Integration. *Journal of Common Market Studies* **10**(3): 267–285.

Puchala, D. (2003). *Theory and History in International Relations*. New York and London, Routledge.

Reus-Smit, C. (2017). Cultural Diversity and International Order. *International Organization* **71**(4): 851–885.

Risse, T., S. C. Ropp and K. Sikkink, Eds. (1999). *The Power of Human Rights: International Norms and Domestic Change*. Cambridge, Cambridge University Press.

Risse, T., S. C. Ropp and K. Sikkink, Eds. (2013). *The Persistent Power of Human Rights: From Commitment to Compliance*. Cambridge, Cambridge University Press.

Ritchie, D. A. (2011). Introduction: The Evolution of Oral History. *The Oxford Handbook of Oral History*. D. A. Ritchie. Oxford, Oxford University Press: 3–22.

Roy, A. and W. J. Starosta (2001). Hans-Georg Gadamer, Language, and Intercultural Communication. *Language and Intercultural Communication* **1**(1): 6–20.

Schmidt, V. A. (2010). Taking Ideas and Discourse Seriously: Explaining Change Through Discursive Institutionalism as the Fourth 'New Institutionalism'. *European Political Science Review* **2**(1): 1–25.

Shore, C. (2000). *Building Europe: The Cultural Politics of European Integration*. London, Routledge.

Sutch, P. and P. Roberts (2019). Outer Space and Neo-Colonial Injustice: Distributive Justice and the Continuous Scramble for Dominium. *International Journal of Social Economics*.

Tallberg, J. (2008). Bargaining Power in the European Council. *Journal of Common Market Studies* **46**(3): 685–708.

Thakur, R. (2011). Nuclear Nonproliferation and Disarmament: Can the Power of Ideas Tame the Power of the State? *International Studies Review* **13**(1): 34–45.

Tiller, R. and E. Nyman (2018). Ocean Plastics and the BBNJ Treaty – Is Plastic Frightening Enough to Insert Itself into the BBNJ Treaty, or Do We Need to Wait for a Treaty of Its Own? *Journal of Environmental Studies and Sciences* **8**(4): 411–415.

Tully, J., Ed. (1988). *Meaning and Context. Quentin Skinner and His Critics*. Princeton, NJ, Princeton University Press.

Wæver, O. (1996). The Rise and Fall of the Inter-Paradigm Debate. *International Theory: Positivism & Beyond*. S. Smith, K. Booth and M. Zalewski. Cambridge, Cambridge University Press: 149–185.

Weldes, J. (1999). *Constructing National Interests – The United States and the Cuban Missile Crisis*. Minneapolis, University of Minnesota Press.

West, M. L. (2007). *Indo-European Poetry and Myth*. Oxford, Oxford University Press.

Wiener, A. (2014). *A Theory of Contestation*. Heidelberg and Berlin, Springer.

Wiener, A. (2018). *Constitution and Contestation of Norms in Global International Relations*. Cambridge, Cambridge University Press.

Wirth, C. (2017). *Danger, Development, and Legitimacy in East Asian Maritime Politics: Securing the Seas Securing the State*. London and New York, Routledge.

Yanow, D. and P. Schwartz-Shea, Eds. (2013). *Interpretation and Method: Emprical Research Methods and the Interpretative Turn*. M. E. Sharpe.

Zürn, M. (2013). Globalization and Global Governance. *Handbook of International Relations*. W. Carlsnaes, T. Risse and B. A. Simmons. London, Sage: 401–425.

Zürn, M. (2018). *A Theory of Global Governance – Authority, Legitimacy & Contestation*. Oxford, Oxford University Press.

Index

abduction 36, 48, 49
action 35, 53
Adler, Emanuel 24, 25
agency 45–46
American Journal of International Law 63
anarchy 3, 4, 62, 73
Arendt, Hannah 89
arguments, topoi 46, 47, 48, 49; *see also* topoi
Aristotle 5
art 22, 30; understanding 35
Assmann, Aleida 31, 88
Attlee administration 4
Austin, John 25

Bakhtin, Mikhail 11
Balkan War 87, 93–94, 101n9; responsibility to protect (RtoP) 97–98; *see also* Kosovo, Germany's participation in
Banerjee, Sanjoy 11
Barthes, Roland 26
Bastian, Gert 92
Beer, Angelika 96
Being 1, 21, 25, 27, 33, 108
Berenskoetter, Felix 30
Bernstein, Richard 30
Bevir, Mark 7, 26
Bildung 30
"Black Sea Region" 11
bounded understanding 30
British-American "special relationship" 4
Bull, Hedley 9
Butler, Judith 24, 25–26

causal relations 7, 44, 46, 48; and constitution 44–45; in global politics 12
Christianity 87
chronotope 47
Cicero 88
Ciuta, Felix 10, 11
civilisation 87
closed waters 68
"Club Voltaires" 91
coexistence 9
cognitive linguistics 53
Cohn-Bendit, Daniel 98
Committee on the Limits of the Continental Shelf (CLCS) 62, 64, 73, 76; and expertocracy 74–75
comparisons 51–52, 52
competent performances 23–25
Comte, August 15, 65, 88
Comtean Positivism 14, 15, 55, 61, 63, 65, 67, 76, 77, 115; expertocracy 73–75, 77; humanity 66, 67, 68–70, 76, 77; objectivity 66, 70–72, 73, 77; Occidental Republic 66; reason 66; social physics 66
concepts 11, 12, 13, 34, 72, 73; abduction 36
conservatism 10
constitution 44, 46, 48; and causation 44–45
constitutive causation 45; *see also* causal relations
constructivist approaches 13, 32, 45, 64; performativity 23
CONTAINER schema 34
context 21, 22
continental margin 72
continental shelf 71; measurement 72, 73, 74
conversations 53
conveying meaning 52, 53
correspondence theory of truth 7, 32; induction 36
Cremer, Ulrich 98
criteria of validity in interpretive research 49–50, 51
critical constructivist approaches 6, 24
Croker, Pete 75
Cruz, Consuelo 11

cultural justice 9
cultural memory 31, 32
culture 3, 5, 21, 22, 34; in global politics 9

Dallmayr, Fred 9
data collection 50, 51
Dayton Agreement 96
declarative knowledge 49
deconstructivist approaches 26
deduction 36
Della Porta, Donatella 51
democratic peace theory 87–88
Descarte, René 35, 43
Dewey, John 10, 22
dialogue, conveying meaning 52, 53
diplomacy: English School approach 10; interpretation 2; "sauna" 3, 4, 6, 14
discourses 3, 7, 10, 24–25; arguments 47; intercultural dialogue 9; narrative 12; rhetoric 28; "strategic narratives" 7
doing, and knowing 25
Doty, Roxanne 25, 26
double hermeneutic 2, 6, 10, 11, 35, 46, 107

Eckersley, Robyn 93
embeddedness 11, 30, 85
embodiment: experience 22, 32–33; mind 32
emotions 3; fear 21–22
'empirical' 49
Enlightenment, the 65; Kant, Immanuel 89
Enloe, Cynthia 7
epigenetics 30–31, 37n7
episteme 5, 28–29, 35
Epp, Roger 10
Epstein, Charlotte 25
ethics 5, 10; phronesis 28–29
European Union (EU) 11
Evensen, Jens 69–70
Evensen group 69–70
experience(s) 11, 30, 35; embodied 22, 32–33; force 33; trauma 31
expertocracy 14, 15, 61, 63, 73–75, 77
explaining 44
explicit memory 30–31

Fabian, Johannes, on performance 28
fear 21–22
feminist approaches 9
finding topoi 54–55
Fischer, Joschka 94, 95, 96, 97, 98
Force, as schema 32–33
foreign policy 111; German 85, 98–99; of the Green Party 93–96; responsibility to protect (RtoP) 83, 84, 86, 88, 97–98, 100n2; *see also* Kosovo, Germany's participation in; responsibility to protect (RtoP)
Foucault, Michel 26
foundationalism 55n1
friendship 3, 4
functional sovereignty 69
"fundies" 92
fusion of horizons xi, 5, 22, 30, 35, 45, 52, 76, 88, 96, 113

Gadamer, Hans-Georg 5, 9, 10, 11, 14, 22, 24, 28, 29, 35, 45, 107, 112
Gane, Mike 66
Garfinkel, Harold 43
Geertz, Clifford 28, 31
gendered issues in global politics 7
genocide 86
German-Russian relations 3, 4, 6, 14
Germany 15, 83; foreign policy 85; Green Party 15, 84, 86, 87, 91, 97, 99; Green Party, foreign policy during the nineties 93–96; nationalism 93–94; "never again war" 93–94, 96; participation in Kosovo 50; participation in Operation Allied Force 84; performances 86; responsibility to protect (RtoP) 83, 84, 86, 88, 97–98; Social Democratic Party 84, 93–94, 97; student movements 91; *see also* Kosovo, Germany's participation in
Glaser, Barry 49
global governance 6, 13, 77, 110, 112, 114, 116
global politics 2, 3, 83, 107, 108, 110; causal relations 12; context 21; and culture 3, 9; democratic peace theory 10; English School approach 10; Eurocentric approaches 7; feminist approaches 9; friendship 4; fusion of horizons 5; gendered issues 7; hermeneutic situations 15; horizons 5, 6, 9, 12, 21, 27, 30, 48; human experience 7; intercultural dialogue 9; meaning 21; models 7; narrative approach 7; narratives 11, 12; performance 22; as politics among people 13; "sauna diplomacy" 4, 6, 14; theories 10; topoi 7, 13
globalisation 9
Goodin, Robert, *Green Political Theory* 93
Gorbachev, Mikhail 3
grand narratives 5
Green Party 15, 84, 86, 87, 91, 97, 99; foreign policy 85; foreign policy

Index

during the nineties 93–96; horizon 85; humanity 91–93; origins 91
Grotius, Hugo 61, 71; *On the Law of War and Peace* 89
Grovogui, Siba 7
Guzzini, Stefano 35

Hague Convention, Martens Clause 89
Hansen, Lene 87
Harrington, John 47
Heidegger, Martin 108
Helfferich, Cornelia 51
hermeneutics 1, 2, 9, 10, 15, 43, 51, 99, 108; *Being* 25; comparisons 51–52; embeddedness 85; and the English School 10; finding topoi 54–55; fusion of horizons 5; horizons 4–5, 29, 30, 44; interpretive approaches 44, 49–50; knowledge 27–30; language 27–30; memory 30–31; performance 6, 12, 21, 22–23, 24, 36, 36–37n2, 44; performativity 25–26; prejudgments 44; sequential analysis 52; topoi 46, 47, 48; UN Convention on the Law of the Sea (UNCLOS) 14
heuristics 51–52
Hinz, Karl 64
historically effective consciousness 5
Hockenos, Paul 92, 97–98
honor/honour 3, 22
horizons 5, 6, 9, 12, 21, 22, 27, 30, 32, 34, 44, 48, 49, 62, 83, 108, 110; fusion of *see 'fusion of horizons'*; of the Green Party 85; prejudgments 29, 32–33, 35; of UNCLOS drafters 72, 73; of Winifred Nachtwei 96
Horizontverschmelzung 30
human agency 32, 45, 45–46, 61, 65, 83, 99, 112
human experience 7
human rights 83, 88–92, 98–100, 110–112
humanism 88–89
humanity 14, 15, 55, 61, 63, 66, 68–70, 76, 83, 85, 86, 87, 100, 110, 115–116; in the Green Party 91, 92–93; in IR 90; and nonviolence 95, 96, 97; and responsibility to protect (RtoP) 97–98, 100n2; selecting as topos 87; and sovereignty 90; as topos for German military intervention in Kosovo 88–89, 90–91
Huntingdon, Samuel 9
Hussein, Saddam 99

identity 11, 14, 23, 25, 85, 87, 98, 100
ideology critique 31
implicit memory 30–31
induction 36
institutions 10, 13
intercultural dialogue 9
internal consistency 51
International Court of Justice (ICJ) 64
international law 3, 62, 88–90, 99
international politics 44; topoi 46
international relations (IR) 1, 2, 3, 4, 76, 83, 99, 110, 114; abductive approach 48; causal approaches 45; constitutive approaches 45; constructivist approaches 32, 64; fusion of horizons 5; hermeneutics 9, 10; horizons 5, 6; humanity 90; interpretive approaches 44, 107–108; and Law of the Sea 62–63; models 7; performance 21–23; as politics among people 14, 64, 85, 86, 111, 112, 114; "practice turn" 21–23; qualitative research 51; scientism 43; securitisation approaches 34; topoi 7; trajectories over time 6; unobservables 3, 13, 43, 107, 111–112, 114, 116; *see also* constructivist approaches; global politics; hermeneutics; topoi
International Seabed Authority (ISA) 62
International Tribune for the Law of the Sea (ITLOS) 62
interpretation 2, 6, 10, 24; and causal relations 7; fear 21–22; performance 21; validity of 50, 51
interpretive approaches 44, 107, 108; criteria of validity in 49–50, 51
interpretive research 46
intersubjectivity 24, 30, 51
Ish-Shalom, Piki 10

Johnson, Mark 22, 26, 32, 33, 113
Johnson, Patrick 36
justice 10; cultural 9

Kane, Anne 11
Kant, Immanuel 35
Kearney, Richard 48
Kelly, Petra 92
knowledge 2, 3, 5, 7, 9, 10, 12, 14, 27–30, 34; abduction 36; creation of 48; declarative 49; and doing 25; *episteme* 5, 28–29, 35; and experience 35; hermeneutic approach 48; horizons 30; interpretation 6; making sense 3;

and meaning 6; new 36; phronesis 5, 28–29, 49; and 'play' 11; and power 26; procedural 49; *techne* 5, 28–29, 35; topoi 46, 47; understanding 35; *see also* meaning; understanding
knowledge production 9
Kohl, Helmut 3
Kollwitz, Käthe 92–94
Kosovo, Germany's participation in 50, 87, 115–116; humanity 88–89, 90–91; responsibility to protect (RtoP) 97–98
Kratochwil, Friedrich 7, 36, 43, 47, 114

Lakoff, George 32, 113
language 10, 12, 21–23, 27–30; conveying meaning 52, 53; force 33; and meaning 24, 26; primary metaphors 34; propositional content 32–33; rhetoric 28; schemas 34; universality of 47; utterances 47; *see also* narrative(s)
Law of the Sea 61, 62, 68, 76, 77, 77n2, 110; and Comtean Positivism 65–67; and expertocracy 73–75; and humanity 67, 68–70; *mare clausum* 72; *mare liberum* 71; objectivity 70–72, 73; as politics among people 62
Lebow, Ned 35, 45
Leibniz, Wilhelm 43
Little, Richard 10
Lynch, Cecelia 7, 36, 49

Machiavelli, Niccolo 88
making sense *see* sense-making
Mann-Borghese, Elizabeth 68
mare clausum 61, 72
mare liberum 61, 71–72
Maren-Grisebach, Manon, *Philosophy of the Greens* 92–93
maritime governance 63; continental shelf 71; and expertocracy 73–75; and humanity 67, 68–70; *mare clausum* 72; *mare liberum* 71; *see also* Law of the Sea; UN Convention on the Law of the Sea (UNCLOS)
Martens Clause 89
Marx, Karl 24, 65
meaning 6, 7, 9, 21, 21–23, 22, 25, 27, 32, 33, 34, 44; conveying 52, 53; and language 24, 26; and neuroscience 32–34; performance 12; and 'play' 11; text 28; topoi 46, 47; and understanding 12–13; *see also* sense-making
Melanchthon, Philip 28

memory 30–31, 34; cultural 31, 32; individual 31; social 31
meta-narratives 55n4
metaphors 53, 113; primary 34
methodology 90, 112–113; hermeneutic 109; interviews 64; literature review 63–64
military interventions: responsibility to protect (RtoP) 83, 84, 86, 88; topoi 87; *see also* Germany; Kosovo, Germany's participation in; Operation Allied Force
Milliken, Jennifer 25
Milosevic, Slobodan 98
models 7
Monahan, D. 73
Moon Treaty 115
Moore, Cerwyn 11
Müller, Kerstin 94, 98

Nachtwei, Winfried 94, 95; horizon 96
narrative(s) 6, 7, 12, 46, 48, 49; causal 45; of identity 11; meta- 55n4; "strategic" 7; topoi 7
national biography 30
nationalism, German 93–94
negotiations, for UNCLOS 69
Neufeld, Mark 9, 10
Neumann, Iver 23, 25, 31
neuroscience 30; and meaning 32–34
Nickels, Christa 95
nomothetic approaches 43
non-governmental organisations (NGOs) 3; humanitarian 90
nonviolence, and responsibility to protect (RtoP) 97–98
norms 3, 7, 32
North Atlantic Treaty, Article 5 84
North Atlantic Treaty Organisation (NATO) 93, 97, 100, 111; "double-track" strategy 92; Operation Allied Force 83–84
Nussbaum, Martha 89

objectivist approaches 43
objectivity 14, 15, 61, 63, 66, 77
Occidental Republic 66
Ocean Development and International Law 63–64
ocean governance 15, 61, 64, 88; continental shelf 71; and expertocracy 73–75; *see also* UN Convention on the Law of the Sea (UNCLOS)
"ongoing accomplishments" 43–44

124 *Index*

Onuf, Nicholas 1, 107
open waters 61, 68
openness 50, 51
Operation Allied Force 83–84
organisations 112
Oslo peace accords 10
Oxman, B. H. 62

Pardo, Arvid 64, 68, 76
performance 108–109; Germany 87
performances 6, 12, 14, 21, 22, 27, 36, 36–37n2, 44, 49–50, 61, 62, 63, 83; Arvid Pardo 68; competent 23–25; context 22; Fabian on 28; finding topoi 54–55; Germany 86; horizons 48; meaning 47; and memory 31–32; "practice turn" 23; social 26; as text 28; and topoi 12–14, 46, 47, 48, 49
performativity 23, 25–26
philosophy 10; Comtean Positivism 65–67; of the Green Party 92–93
phronesis 5, 28–29, 49; functional dimension 29
Platzöder, Renate 64
'play' 11
"play of performances" 6
politics: hermeneutic approach 48; topoi 46
positioning analysis 53
positivist approaches 1, 7, 10, 24, 49, 50, 56n13, 66; *see also* Comtean Positivism
poststructuralism 32; performativity 25–26
Pouliot, Vincent 24, 25, 51
power 7, 12, 24; and knowledge 26
"practice turn" 21–23, 26; competent performances 23–25; discourses 25; phronesis 28–29
praxis 10, 11
predicate analysis 53
prejudgments 5, 22, 29, 32–33, 35, 44; comparisons 52
prejudices 5, 29, 37n3
primary metaphors 34
problem-based theory building 44, 49, 64, 114
procedural knowledge 49
propositional content 32–33

qualitative research 51

Rattray, Ken 69
"real world" 7
"realos" 92
reason 66; and meaning 32

reflected and directed action 25
region-building 10, 11; "Black Sea Region" 11
Renaissance humanism 88–89
representational practices 7
research 55; qualitative 51; *see also* hermeneutics; methodology
responsibility to protect (RtoP) 83, 84, 86, 88, 97–98, 99, 100n2, 100n4
rhetoric 28; topoi 46, 47
Rhodes, Rod 7, 26
Ricœur, Paul 10, 11, 14, 24, 30, 32, 35, 48, 112
Roth, Claudia 94
Ruggie, John 45, 48–49

Saco, Diane 24
Sanger, Clyde 64
"sauna diplomacy" 3, 4, 6, 14
schemas 34
scientism 43
security 10
Selden, John 61
semantics 53
sense-making 1, 2, 3, 6, 7, 21, 27, 33–34, 48, 48–49; and phronesis 5; text 28
sequential analysis 51–52
Shapcott, Richard 9, 10
Skinner, Quentin 112
Social Democratic Party 93–94, 97
social imaginaries 21, 46
social memory 31
social performances 26
social physics 66
sociology, knowledge-based approaches 35
Somers, Margaret 11
sovereignty 7, 67, 83, 93, 101n16; functional 69; German 94–95; and humanity 90; oceans 61; and responsibility to protect (RtoP) 85–86
Space Law 77, 115
speech-acts 25; conversations 53; semantics 53
standing 22
state(s) 4, 13, 21, 26, 85, 112; roles 22; *see also* sovereignty
Steinberg, Philip 61
Stevenson, Jack 62, 70
"strategic narratives" 7
Strauss, Anselm 49
student movements in Germany 91

Taylor, Charles 10, 21, 48, 112
techne 5, 28–29, 35

Teitel, Ruti 89
text: conveying meaning 52, 53; as performance 28; sequential analysis 52; UN Convention on the Law of the Sea (UNCLOS) 69
theatre analogy of performances 22
theories 10, 12, 113
Third Debate in International Relations 109
Thompson-Flores, Sergio 70
throwness of *Being* 29
topoi 7, 12, 13, 46, 47, 48, 49, 51, 56n7, 64, 112, 113; Comtean Positivism 63; expertocracy 73–75; finding 54–55; German foreign policy 83; humanity 67, 68–70, 83, 85, 86, 87, 88–89, 90–91, 100, 110, 115–116; for military interventions 87; objectivity 70–72, 73; and performance 12–14
transcultural dialogue 9
trauma 31
Trittin, Jürgen 94
Truman administration 4, 71
Truman Proclamation 71, 76
trust 3, 4, 14
Tully, James 112
Turner, Victor 28, 36–37n2

UN Charter, Chapter VII 84
UN Committee on the Peaceful Use of Outer Space (COPUOS) 115
UN Convention on the Law of the Sea (UNCLOS) 14, 50, 61, 62, 76, 83, 110, 113; Article 76 63, 72, 74; Article 76.4 72; and Comtean Positivism 65–67; Evensen group 69–70; and expertocracy 73–75; horizons of drafters 72, 73; and humanity 67, 68–70; *mare liberum* 71–72; negotiations 69; objectivity 70–72, 73

understanding 2, 12, 27, 29, 35, 44; art 35; bounded 30; comparisons 52; conveying meaning 52, 53; horizons 52; and meaning 12–13; performance 12; through textual sources 11
United Kingdom 3; *see also* British-American "special relationship"
United Nations, Universal Declaration of Human Rights 90
United States 3; *see also* British-American "special relationship"
Universal Declaration of Human Rights 90
universality of language 47
unobservables 3, 13, 21, 43, 107, 111–112, 114, 116
utterances 25, 47; arguments 47

validity of interpretations 49–50, 51
values 7

Waltz, Kenneth 3; *Theory of International Politics* 43
warfare 1, 101n12; Martens Clause 89; *see also* Balkan War; Kosovo, Germany's participation in
Warnke, Georgia 30
Watt, David 4
Weber, Max 35
Weldes, Jutta 24–25
Wendt, Alexander 25, 44
Wight, Martin 9
Wittgenstein, Ludwig 24, 47, 112
Wolf, Klaus Dieter 71

Yankov, Alexander 70
Yeltsin, Boris 3
Yugoslavia 85; *see also* Operation Allied Force

Zürn, Michael 114